NEW DIRECTIONS FOR TEACHING AND LEARNING

Robert J. Menges, *Northwestern University*
EDITOR-IN-CHIEF

Marilla D. Svinicki, *University of Texas, Austin*
ASSOCIATE EDITOR

D0271157

College Teaching:
From Theory to Practice

Robert J. Menges
Northwestern University

Marilla D. Svinicki
University of Texas, Austin

EDITORS

Number 45, Spring 1991

JOSSEY-BASS INC., PUBLISHERS
San Francisco

COLLEGE TEACHING: FROM THEORY TO PRACTICE
Robert J. Menges, Marilla D. Svinicki (eds.)
New Directions for Teaching and Learning, no. 45
Robert J. Menges, Editor-in-Chief

Microfilm copies of issues and articles are available in 16mm and 35mm,
as well as microfiche in 105mm, through University Microfilms Inc., 300
North Zeeb Road, Ann Arbor, Michigan 48106.

LC 85-644763   ISSN 0271-0633   ISBN 1-55542-799-5

NEW DIRECTIONS FOR TEACHING AND LEARNING is part of The Jossey-
Bass Higher and Adult Education Series and is published quarterly by
Jossey-Bass Inc., Publishers. Second-class postage paid at San Francisco,
California, and at additional mailing offices. Postmaster: Send address
changes to Jossey-Bass Inc., Publishers, 350 Sansome Street, San Fran-
cisco, California 94104.

EDITORIAL CORRESPONDENCE should be sent to Robert J. Menges, Northwestern University, Center for the Teaching Professions, 2003 Sheridan
Road, Evanston, Illinois 60208-2610.

Cover photograph by Richard Blair/Color & Light © 1990.

Printed on acid-free paper in the United States of America.

CONTENTS

From the New Editors

Since 1980, *New Directions for Teaching and Learning* has brought a unique blend of theory, research, and practice to leaders in postsecondary education. As we begin our editorship of the series, we feel honored to follow Kenneth Eble, Jack Noonan, and Robert Young. They established a publication noted not only for its substance but also for its timeliness, compactness, and accessibility.

During the 1990s, our editorial policies will continue to emphasize significant new directions for teaching and learning in postsecondary education. In particular, we hold these goals for the series:

1. To inform about current and future trends in teaching and learning
2. To elaborate the context that shapes those trends
3. To illustrate those trends through examples from real settings
4. To propose how those trends can be implemented in new settings.

By providing serious analyses of instruction in higher education, this publication reflects our view that teaching deserves respect as a high form of scholarship. We believe that significant scholarship is done not only by the researcher who reports results of studies but also by the practitioner who shares with others disciplined reflections on teaching. Contributors to the series will approach questions of teaching and learning as seriously as they approach substantive questions in their own disciplines, including examination of the intellectual and social context out of which these questions arise. Authors will deal with both theory and research and with practice, and they will translate from research and theory to practice and back again. We believe our own backgrounds are consistent with the goals of the series. One editor works primarily in research and the other primarily in practice.

As researcher and writer, Robert J. Menges has been a regular contributor to the literature about how college teaching is conducted and evaluated. He is a professor of education and social policy at Northwestern University and has been affiliated with Northwestern's Center for the Teaching Professions for nearly twenty years. In 1988, he published (with Claude Mathis) *Key Resources for Teaching, Learning, Curriculum, and Faculty Development.* He currently directs the research program on faculty and instruction of the National Research and Development Center for Postsecondary Teaching, Learning, and Assessment. As a researcher, he values scholarship that effectively informs practice; as an editor, he values writing that speaks clearly to practitioners, as well as to researchers; and as a teacher, he values encounters that celebrate both the joys and the hard work of teaching and learning.

Marilla D. Svinicki has been in the trenches of teaching and faculty development since 1974, viewing college classes as a student, a teacher, and an observer. As director of the Center for Teaching Effectiveness at the University of Texas, Austin, she struggles side by side with students and faculty to make sense of the processes of teaching and learning in everyday situations. She has also taught these processes in her own graduate classes in educational psychology, a forum where research and practice must be blended, and she confesses that her students are often the guinea pigs for procedures that she derives from theory and wants to test before recommending to others. As a former executive director of the Professional and Organizational Development Network in Higher Education, she has influenced national trends in faculty development.

The intended audience for this series includes faculty, administrators, and other policymakers in higher education, members of professional development committees, personnel in instructional development agencies, staff members at learning-support services, and researchers studying postsecondary education. We ask your assistance in bringing the series to the attention of new readers, especially when the topic of an issue matches the interests of someone you know.

In summary, we intend *New Directions for Teaching and Learning* to discuss the theory and research behind new practices, to offer reflections on problems that teachers and learners face, to describe possible solutions, and to provide close scrutiny of research, practice, and the links between research and practice. We believe that no other publication can achieve these purposes as well, because no other publication serves the same combination of audiences in quite this way. This publication serves as a unique meeting place for researchers and practitioners. We invite your comments on the series to date and your suggestions for its future.

Robert J. Menges
Editor-in-Chief

Marilla D. Svinicki
Associate Editor

PREFACE

College teachers face an enormous number of choices as they plan and carry out instruction. The three most critical choices concern what should be taught, how it should be taught, and how we will know if it has been taught. Over the years, great effort has been invested in the first area—witness the extensive debates about core curricula. Recently, much attention has been devoted to the third—witness the assessment movement in higher education.

In this volume, we direct attention to the second—choices about how teaching should be conducted. How we teach is often little more than a replication of how we were taught, an imitation apparently based on the belief that our students will thrive under the same conditions that were effective for us. Or excellence in teaching is credited to mysterious inborn talents. To be sure, some teachers do have natural gifts, just as some musicians have perfect pitch. But most have to practice as hard to become experts in pedagogy as to become experts in a discipline. Even teachers with natural talent can further excel by understanding the processes underlying teaching and learning, just as great musicians must understand the principles of composition and esthetic expression. Without such understanding, teachers are susceptible to the quick fix of "rules for good teaching." But teaching by rules is no more appropriate for a teacher than painting by numbers is for an artist. Growth and development come from deep understanding of teaching and learning, rather than from slavish imitations of former teachers, reliance on innate ability, or conformity to prescribed rules.

Understanding the processes of teaching and learning is possible for all, but searching for that knowledge can be daunting. Only an intrepid few search out scholarship on teaching and attempt to apply its findings, and they are often disappointed by what they discover. Educational literature is no more accessible to nonspecialists than is the literature of any other field. The educational literature includes scattered sources difficult to locate, competing theories difficult to evaluate, and jargon difficult to translate. This issue of *New Directions for Teaching and Learning* attempts to draw interesting and useful information into one place, in a form that can be readily understood and applied.

We begin with theories because theories, whether formal or informal, influence how instructors relate to students, how they deal with subject matter, and even how they regard themselves. Theories of teaching and learning are useful because they help instructors evaluate information. They inform practice and spark innovation. Moreover, knowledge of today's theory helps shape future theory and action. As practicing professionals, instructors want to know about theories as the basis for what they do. As pragmatists, instructors find that theories can actually help them become better at what they do.

This volume elaborates three theoretical perspectives through which teaching can be viewed and explores their implications for the practice of teaching. These theoretical perspectives are the cognitive, which deals primarily with strategies by which information is processed; the motivational, which deals primarily with how learning is initiated and sustained; and the social, which examines the interpersonal context of teaching and learning.

The opening chapter discusses the natural human tendency to view the world through one's personal theory, a theory that is usually implicit. The authors examine how implicit theories are often misleading, how they can be made explicit through reflection, and how they can be blended with more formal theories.

A pair of chapters is then devoted to each perspective. The first chapter of each pair presents current concepts and research underlying the respective theory. It discusses key assumptions, generative models that can be applied to instructional planning, and concepts useful for thinking about problems in teaching. The second chapter in the pair translates the theory into more practical terms, including applications to everyday problems of typical instructors.

No single perspective, however, can explain all that goes on in an instructional situation. Because instructors must learn to use alternating or combined perspectives, the final chapter discusses how instructors can weave multiple perspectives together to meet instructional challenges and solve instructional problems. The chapter analyzes instructional situations—from each perspective, considered separately, and in light of the three combined.

This volume also offers a framework into which readers may incorporate developments in educational theory and research that they subsequently encounter in their professional activities. We hope that these chapters will persuade readers to reflect on the rationales behind their instructional choices and to review those choices in light of research-based theories.

Robert J. Menges
Marilla D. Svinicki
Editors

Robert J. Menges is professor of education and social policy at Northwestern University and director of the research program on faculty and instruction of the National Research and Development Center for Postsecondary Teaching, Learning, and Assessment.

Marilla D. Svinicki is director of the Center for Teaching Effectiveness, University of Texas, Austin.

Personal theories about teaching and learning are often implicit and likely to be inaccurate. When implicit theories become explicit, they can blend with formal theories to improve the practice of teaching.

How Practice Is Shaped by Personal Theories

William C. Rando, Robert J. Menges

College teaching has its share of surprises. Some are pleasant—a smile of understanding replaces a student's puzzled frown, a provocative discussion question sets the class buzzing, an unexpected insight turns up in a student's essay. Some surprises are not so pleasant—class attendance drops suddenly, a student poses a question that the teacher cannot answer, several students' papers look suspiciously similar.

We cope with events like these and the surprises they bring by relying on personal theories about teaching and learning. Although primitive in comparison with formal theory, personal theories serve to bring some regularity to experience. They put intellectual structure around our worlds of teaching and learning.

Many personal theories are implicit; that is, they lie outside awareness, and they are divorced from the more structured knowledge contained in formal theories. In this chapter, we discuss the characteristics of implicit theories, how implicit theories can become explicit, and how personal theories can blend with formal theories.

Conceptualizing Implicit Theories

Implicit theories are our individual submerged rationales about events in the world and about our own behavior in the world. Sometimes events cause us to try to explain something that we "never really thought about before." We may discover that, on the basis of tacit or implicit knowledge, we can come up with explanations after all: in our process of thinking and explaining our implicit theories have become explicit. Different researchers

NEW DIRECTIONS FOR TEACHING AND LEARNING, no. 45, Spring 1991 © Jossey-Bass Inc., Publishers and theorists describe implicit theories in distinctive ways. In this section, we consider three representative conceptualizations of implicit theories.

Implicit Theories as Scripts. Several researchers in the communication sciences employ the term *script* to describe the tacit knowledge used in everyday social interaction (Roloff and Berger, 1982). Existing outside our awareness, scripts are like little plays we act out on cue. The cue may be an internal impulse or, more likely, something in the external world. For teachers, the familiar event of a student asking about a grade may cue a "when students ask about grades" script. This script, like other implicit theories, serves an immediate function that is positive. It helps us cope with a situation that otherwise would be surprising and produce anxiety. In the long run, however, the script may not be effective, since it pops up automatically and we read from it even in inappropriate situations.

A faculty member who became aware of her grading script realized that it was always cued when a student wanted to discuss grades. Through reflection, she discovered that the script originated in her early college experiences, when she came to believe that students who approached professors about grades gained an unfair advantage over less assertive students. As a college teacher, she now views students who want to talk about grades as manipulative. The following conversation, reconstructed by the teacher, between her and a student shows the script at work, both in what she says and in how she thinks about the interaction (her thoughts are shown in brackets):

STUDENT: I'd like to ask you about the grading of this homework.

TEACHER: O.K. What's the problem? [Another grade grubber.]

STUDENT: Here, on this problem, you took off five points.

TEACHER: Yes, I see that. And? [Hold your temper.]

STUDENT: Well, five points seems like a lot to take off when I only made this one little mistake.

TEACHER: I guess you got nailed! (Laughs.) [Whoops! Tried to make a joke that wasn't taken at all well.] Hey, only joking. Seriously, I took five points off all papers that had the mistake. A lot of people made this mistake, and I took five off each time. [O.K. Let's see if the standard "you aren't alone" argument will work in this situation.]

STUDENT: Well, I think that's unfair. Five points for such a little thing. Come on!

The instructor's script put her on the defensive. The student's final comment reveals his dissatisfaction with the outcome.

Implicit Theories as Syllogisms. Argyris (1985) frames implicit theories as logical syllogisms or "if . . . then" propositions. So defined, implicit theories are thought to be based on assumptions about facts and about relationships of those facts in the world. Some propositions are quite general; others, like the following, are situationally specific: "Students tune out when instructors bore them. These students of mine are tuned out. Therefore, I must be boring." Such propositions bring regularity to our interpretations of experience and may lead us to adopt consistent coping strategies, but they are not necessarily accurate. Like scripts, syllogisms may lead to unexamined reactions.

Implicit Theories as Broad Orientations to Teaching. Some educational theorists conceptualize implicit theories more broadly, as orientations to the tasks of teaching. Using metaphorical language, Fox (1983, p. 152) described several theories derived from interviews with new polytechnic teachers in England, many of whom—like the chemistry professor who said his job was to "give the elements of physical chemistry to students"—talked about students as if they were vessels waiting to be filled. Fox calls this the "transfer" theory. Other teachers regarded students as clay or wood to be molded, carved, or otherwise transformed (the "shaping" theory). Fox considers these to be "simple" theories because in them the teacher is active and the student is passive.

By contrast, teachers with more experience were likely to hold more developed and complex theories, theories that acknowledge the activity of the student as well as the activity of the teacher. For example, some teachers saw themselves as guides over the terrain of subject matter, which students and teachers traverse together (the "traveling" theory).

In another study (Menges and Rando, 1989), the language of graduate teaching assistants (TAs) revealed three orientations to teaching. When TAs were asked what they meant by the term *teaching,* their responses reflected either orientation toward content, orientation toward process, or orientation toward motivation. One example of a content-oriented response is "Teaching is my giving them knowledge and their understanding and being able to apply it." Responses showing the process orientation are "Teaching is making people think for themselves" and "To teach is to help someone teach himself." A typical response oriented toward motivation is "The first priority seems to be to interest students in the subject." These orientations also correlated with how TAs said they handled classroom problems. Since orientations are typically implicit, however, they may not influence all situations in a consistent way.

Whether implicit theories are conceived as scripts, as syllogisms, or as broad orientations to teaching, they serve to guide practice. As the grading script illustrates, that guidance may be inaccurate and counterproductive. Implicit theories are outside our awareness, and the assumptions on which they are founded are taken for granted. We are no more likely to verify them than we are to check the air before we breathe or the ground before we move our feet. Unfortunately, unlike the air and the ground, implicit theories are our own creations and prone to error.

Inaccuracies in Implicit Theories

If we create our own implicit theories, why do they not necessarily match the real world more closely? One answer to this question is that implicit theories are essentially protective. We generate them to provide a rationale for the world and for our actions. Without their protection, we would be overwhelmed by the anxiety caused by ambiguity and change. Implicit theories impart structure and stability to our experience. We willingly trade accurate perceptions about the world's complexity and idiosyncrasy for the comfort of manageable simplicity. Because our theories vastly oversimplify complex matters, they often carry distortions and embody logical compromises.

A second reason for less-than-accurate implicit theories is that we create them subconsciously, rather than thoughtfully. Over the years, one may come to believe implicitly that male students are smarter than female students or that a student's pattern of interaction means that he is being manipulative. These assumptions can influence how we design courses or interact with students, and the results only reconfirm our original theories. The process of circular confirmation allows inaccurate implicit theories to grow in strength and number.

A third explanation for the inaccuracy of implicit theories is drawn from critical theory. According to critical theorists (Giroux, 1983; Kemmis, 1985), cultural norms and institutional practices embody implicit theories. These theories are sustained at a level beyond the individual, in the ideologies of institutions and societies. For example, part of the ideology of colleges and universities involves the maintenance of academic standards through rigorous grading. Teachers may deal with such matters passively rather than critically, becoming dependent, over time, on the ideologies they have tacitly created. These dependencies sometimes lead to conflict, as teachers simultaneously defend the institution and feel oppressed by its practices; thus instructors may defend the importance of academic standards even as they feel oppressed by the grading system under which they work.

In day-to-day social interactions, implicit theories serve to free mental energy for other activities or for relaxation. When we must make skilled judgments based on accurate information, however, our dependence on the implicit and the untested may result in poor professional practice. Exasperated questions—"How did I end up here?" "What do I do now?"— are probably the result of following some implicit theory of behavior, rather than testing an explicit version of the theory.

A scenario of error can play itself out during a class meeting, leaving the teacher befuddled after the class is over. The scenario may persist over years, rather than days, and leave the teacher bitter or disheartened and sensing many lost opportunities. Implicit theories and untested assumptions ultimately can have an oppressive effect on the ability to grow, change, and reconcile new experiences. One central justification for attending to our implicit theories is that we develop, as educators and as individuals, through the process of questioning basic assumptions and theories.

Making Explicit What Has Been Implicit

How are implicit theories explicated? Some suggestions come from experiential learning theory. Kolb (1984) discusses contributions to experiential learning theory by Dewey, Lewin, and Piaget, as well as his own work on this topic. All these approaches emphasize reflection, and reflection requires thinking about behavior in a way that uncovers what was formerly hidden. Reflection permits us to learn from experience, rather than merely to receive experience passively or respond to it automatically. Not all experience produces or inspires reflection, although all experience can be reflected on. Unfortunately, we often circumvent real reflection through superficial justi- — fication and self-defense. In an educational setting, feedback from others can help to elicit our reflection by exposing our defensive routines and encouraging more rigorous questioning. Both Dewey's reflective-thinking steps and Kolb's experiential learning cycle entail constant questioning.

When we reflect on our experience, our implicit theories become apparent, even transparent. Having been explicated, implicit theories and the behaviors they produce become part of what we can think about and experience directly. We are then able to use these theories productively, perhaps in combination with more formal theories. They become vehicles for improving our practice, rather than mere determinants of our reflexive behavior.

On the basis of a process of reflection and questioning, Menges (1990) suggests how faculty discussion groups can uncover implicit theories. Participants would routinely follow four steps: articulate a belief about teaching, identify a problematic teaching situation, report the behavior intended to resolve the problem, and find a rationale that links the belief and the behavior. Under the scrutiny of group discussion, much that has been implicit comes into awareness, where it can be examined. For example, a teacher of history may assert her belief that only when students compare and contrast assigned readings, by discussing them in class, do they master the skills of complex reasoning about history. When she asks students to do this in class, however, she says that her questions are greeted with silence. Colleagues in the discussion group suggest that a videotape of one of her classes may be revealing. On the basis of the tape, she decides that she may not be giving the students enough time to formulate their responses before she breaks the silence by answering her own questions. She resolves to pause longer after posing questions, and to give students some suggestions about managing comparison-contrast questions. As her theory becomes explicit, she extends it to include speculations about why students behave as they do: they need more time for higher-order thinking. She may also be ready to explore formal cognitive theories and to select cognitive learning strategies (like those discussed in Chapters Two and Three) that can be blended with her personal theories.

When collegial discussions of this kind are extended to include formal theories about teaching and learning, the group can examine relationships among implicit theories, formal theories, and behavior. Discussion may even reveal resistances and biases that members hold about formal educational theories. Group discussions can address inconsistencies and explore how they can be resolved.

Blending Personal and Formal Theories

College teachers may encounter formal theories in their reading or at workshops and other meetings. New information from formal theories is inevitably interpreted in light of personal theories, whether the personal theories are implicit or explicit.

Research with precollege teachers finds important differences between formal theories of education, which are conveyed by textbooks, and personal theories, which are held by individual teachers (Pinnegar and Carter, 1990). In textbooks, theories about teaching and learning present the *discipline* (usually educational psychology); for teachers, theories explain individual *experience*. Compared with textbook theories, teachers' theories often lack specificity and definition. Teachers' theories also give prominence to concepts that are absent from textbook theories, such as the role of intuition in teaching. Moreover, teachers often posit relationships among concepts that textbook authors do not. For example, several teachers in the Pinnegar and Carter (1990) study revealed an implicit theory that incorporated the concepts of confidence, trust, and success. This theory, put briefly, states that students can sense when teachers feel confident about themselves and their work, that students are more likely to trust a confident teacher, and that students' trust in the teacher increases the chances of their attempting the work set by the teacher and thereby increases the likelihood of their academic success. Textbook theories, however, did not connect those concepts.

Despite these differences between personal and formal theories, we believe that the two can be blended. Figure 1 depicts this process schematically. Personal theories are depicted as cloudlike in Figure 1 because they are often ambiguous and tentative. Implicit theories are shown with a direct connection to practice. When they become explicit, through processes like those already discussed, they cross the border into awareness. Thus theories can be consciously examined before they influence action.

Figure 1. Blending Personal and Formal Theories to Influence Practice

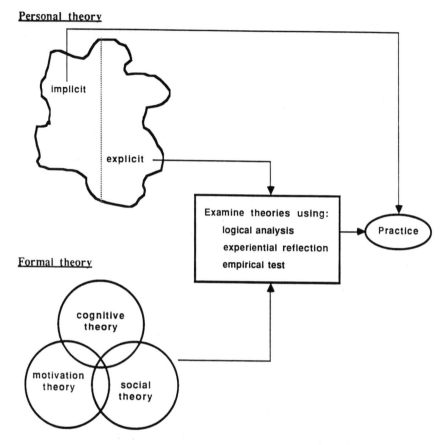

Formal theories, such as those presented in the subsequent chapters of this volume, are by definition explicit and available for examination. They can be examined and blended in a number of ways, three of which are listed in Figure 1. First, both personal and formal theories can be analyzed according to the conventions of logic, an activity that faculty members find challenging. Second, both kinds of theory can be evaluated for consistency with personal experience, an approach especially useful when groups of faculty members reflect together on their experiences. Third, they can be tested empirically through application and evaluation in the classroom.

Conclusion

We believe that every college teacher has a professional obligation to formulate and articulate a rationale for his or her instructional world. Developing that rationale requires reflection about personal theories, knowledge of formal theories, and blending of the personal and the formal. In this chapter, we have elaborated the characteristics of implicit and explicit personal theories. The following chapters turn to formal theories, discussing both their content and their applications to instruction.

References

Argyris, C. *Action Science*. San Francisco: Jossey-Bass, 1985.

Fox, D. "Personal Theories of Teaching." *Studies in Higher Education*, 1983, *8*, 141–163.

Giroux, H. A. *Theory and Resistance in Education: A Pedagogy for the Opposition*. Exeter, N.H.: Heinemann, 1983.

Kemmis, S. "Action Research and the Politics of Reflection." In D. Boud, R. Keogh, and D. Walker (eds.), *Reflection: Turning Experience into Learning*. London: Kogan Page, 1985.

Kolb, D. *Experiential Learning*. Englewood Cliffs, N.J.: Prentice-Hall, 1984.

Menges, R. J. "Teaching: Beliefs and Behaviors." *Teaching Excellence*, 1990, 2 (6), 1–2.

Menges, R. J., and Rando, W. C. "What Are Your Assumptions? Improving Instruction by Examining Theories." *College Teaching*, 1989, 37, 54–60.

Pinnegar, S., and Carter, K. "Comparing Theories from Textbooks and Practicing Teachers." *Journal of Teacher Education*, 1990, 41, 20–27.

Roloff, M. E., and Berger, C. R. (eds.). *Social Cognition and Communication*. Newbury Park, Calif.: Sage, 1982.

William C. Rando is a doctoral candidate at Northwestern University and coordinator of faculty development at Northwestern's University College.

Robert J. Menges is professor of education and social policy at Northwestern University and director of the research program on faculty and instruction of the National Research and Development Center for Postsecondary Teaching, Learning, and Assessment.

College instructors should focus their teaching not only on content but also on how to learn content in the context of particular courses.

PCK?

Cognitive Learning Strategies and College Teaching

Claire E. Weinstein, Debra K. Meyer

Cognitive psychology eludes precise definition. The term encompasses a family of approaches, models, methodologies, and data sets. There is no one cognitive perspective, but rather a variety of approaches, each of which attempts to explain a particular aspect of human behavior (see Anderson, 1980; Collins and Smith, 1988; Gardner, 1985; Knapp, 1986; Mayer, 1981). As in all families, some members get along better than others, not all are interested in the same areas, some are very popular, and some are quite eccentric. And, as with the differences of opinion that occur among family members, there is disagreement among cognitive psychologists on a definition for the field, as well as on its derivation. Given such confusion and disagreement, it is difficult to present a concise definition and a fully integrated paradigm to guide instructional research, development, and implementation. Instead, we use cognitive psychology as a general theme to capture much of the research and theory development that is most directly relevant to postsecondary instruction and learning.

The Central Theme of Cognitive Psychology

Cognitive psychology is the study of how cognitions (thoughts and mental processes) influence other cognitions and behaviors. Furthermore, cognitive psychologists are interested in the processes and mechanisms by which these influences take place. Learners can use many cognitive processes to help take active control of their own learning. To understand the processes that learners can use to control their own thoughts and behaviors, it is useful first to understand how people take in and process information in order to make it available for later access and use.

All of us constantly use our senses to take in information from the outside world. We constantly recall things from memory. These two sources of information are combined in an information-processing center (IPC) in the mind. This center is like a conference table on which we lay out information from our own thoughts and from the outside world. Once we have information in this IPC, we can examine, analyze, or evaluate it, so that we can decide what we want to remember from these conference activities and what we may want to do as a result of the deliberations. The material we remember after the conference activities are over is held in what is referred to as *long-term memory*. This is the file used to hold our knowledge. The better the file is organized, the more easily information can be retrieved from it in the future.

In reality, memory is best described as a continuum, ranging from short-term memory to long-term memory. When we call the operator to get the phone number of a local restaurant where we want to have dinner, we often repeat the number over and over while dialing. We are keeping this information in the short-term end of the memory continuum because we need to remember it only long enough to dial the seven digits. As we move along the memory continuum, we hold on to the new information for longer and longer periods and find it easier to remember and use. If we need to pick up a spouse's birthday gift, we want to remember this information until we get to the store and pick up the present. However, we do not want to remember this information forever. Moving along the continuum, we want to remember information about where our classes meet each semester, and we want to remember it for the entire semester. Much farther along the continuum is the important information that we want to remember for a very long time, such as major principles in our field.

To move information along the memory continuum requires some work. We must generate connections between the information we are trying to learn and the knowledge already organized in our memory file. The more connections we can generate, and the more meaningful those connections are, the more meaning we can create for the new information, and the easier it will be to hold on to and access in the future. This is why concepts from an introductory course often seem more difficult to learn than those in an advanced course. In an introductory course, we have little prior knowledge about the topic or field, and what we do have is often poorly organized and integrated. This makes it difficult to use what we already know in making sense of the new information. The more prior knowledge we have in an area or a field of study, and the more this knowledge is organized and integrated, the more we can make sense of new information that we are trying to learn, and the more connections we can build between it and what we already know.

This connecting and organizing goes on in the IPC all the time, but the conference table of the IPC has limited space and cannot hold everything we know or need to know at the same time. To work efficiently, we need to use executive processes to control the flow of information. These include thinking about our goal(s) for the conference or task at hand, deciding what is important to remember and for how long, choosing a strategy for helping us to remember the information, implementing the strategy, monitoring its effectiveness, changing the strategy as necessary, and evaluating the overall outcome when we are done. These processes make it possible to move old and new information into and out of the IPC and the memory continuum, so that we can function efficiently in our complex environment.

Cognitive Strategies

This concept of executive processes leads directly to the perspective on cognitive learning strategies from which this chapter is written. A *cognitive learning strategy* is a plan for orchestrating cognitive resources, such as attention and long-term memory, to help reach a learning goal.

Cognitive learning strategies have several characteristics in common. First, they are *goal-directed*. Learning strategies are used to help meet a standard of performance or to reach a learning goal. Second, cognitive learning strategies are *intentionally invoked*, which implies at least some level of active selection. The selection of one or more of these strategies is determined by a number of factors, such as students' prior experience with a strategy, prior experience with similar learning tasks, ability to deal with distractions, and commitment to goals. Third, cognitive learning strategies are *effortful*; they require time and often involve using multiple, highly interactive steps. Because of the effort required, students must be motivated to initiate and maintain strategy use. In addition, students must believe that the strategy will be effective and that they can be successful using the strategy. Finally, cognitive learning strategies are not universally applicable; they are *situation-specific*. One's goals, the task requirements, the context, and so forth, all interact to help determine which strategy may be best. To be successful in selecting and using a strategy, students must understand under what circumstances a given strategy is or is not appropriate.

Students' Cognitive Strategies for Learning

To select or create strategies that will help students meet their learning goals, students must be aware of characteristics about themselves as learners (also referred to as *self characteristics*), they must know about the characteristics of the tasks they are expected to perform, and they must know about different types of learning strategies. What students know about their own strengths and weaknesses as learners, and what they know about the nature and requirements of different learning tasks, interacts with their knowledge of learning strategies, to help them select and use appropriate strategies both effectively and efficiently. Thus, decisions about how to learn evolve from a number of factors related to the executive processes already described.

Strategies are used to help students reach goals. Information about themselves as learners and about task parameters is essential for setting specific, realistic, challenging goals. For example, if a student (*self charac-teristics*) knows very little about the history of the Vietnam conflict, does not enjoy studying history, finds it difficult to study subjects he does not like, often does poorly on essay exams, and (*task characteristics*) knows the upcoming test is going to be an essay exam requiring the integration of the material presented in the class discussions and in the appropriate textbook chapters, it would be unrealistic for him to set a goal of getting an A on the upcoming history midterm. Given what this student knows about himself and the task, it might be more realistic but still challenging for him to set a goal of B- on the exam. Setting unrealistically high goals does not usually help one reach them. In fact, unrealistically high goals may set up a failure that makes it even harder to perform the next time a similar situation arises.

Because strategies are actively selected by the learner, the success of a strategy also depends on how well it fits both the self and the task charac-teristics. The history student just described needs to use strategies that will help him overcome his lack of background knowledge (perhaps by linking new information to be learned with already familiar information, even if it is from other periods of history or from other disciplines) and his lack of understanding about how to take essay tests (perhaps by creating a glossary of verbs commonly used in essay questions and outlining typical answer structures for questions using these verbs). Another student may not have the same learning needs or the same poor task understanding. She may use different strategies that more closely reflect her understanding of herself as a learner and her understanding of the task. It is easier to be motivated both to start and to finish an academic task if we believe that we can be successful and are motivated to reach the goal.

Finally, because effective strategies are situation-specific, they can be chosen only within the constraints of the individual and the environment. Therefore, both the self and the task characteristics must be taken into account in selecting appropriate learning strategies for any specific learning context.

Students' Knowledge About Themselves as Learners. Two important types of self-knowledge are knowledge about how we learn and knowledge about our prior knowledge of the content or subject being studied. To be effective, students need to be aware of themselves as learners. How reflective are they about themselves as learners? How tuned in are they to themselves as students? Successful students know a lot about themselves. For example, they know which learning styles they prefer, which subjects are easier or more difficult for them to learn, how school fits in with their personal, occupational, and social goals, and what their best and worst times of day are for studying.

In addition to knowing about themselves as learners, effective students also think about their prior content knowledge. The term *prior knowledge* refers to the knowledge that students bring to a particular learning task. To be truly useful, knowledge must be organized and integrated in a meaningful way. Recalling and using what they already know about a subject area can help students add meaning to what they are trying to learn, as well as help them store related topics together. As noted earlier, relating new information to prior knowledge not only aids immediate learning but also helps move things from the IPC to long-term storage, so that it can be used in the future. Thus students in an advanced course already have a large knowledge base to use in building connections to the new information they are trying to learn. Being aware of this fact, and using it to select appropriate learning strategies, is an example of the value of self-knowledge.

Students' Knowledge About Course Context and Learning Tasks. Along with knowing about themselves as learners and being aware of their prior knowledge in a subject, students also need to know about the characteristics of the course context and the learning tasks. A large lecture class in art history has characteristics very different from a small discussion section in medical ethics. The dynamics of a seminar class can vary tremendously according to the discussion leader and the participants.

In any particular course, students also need to be aware of specific task requirements. For example, not knowing about different text structures or about how to identify important information in a textbook can make completing class reading assignments almost impossible. Students need to understand what different academic tasks—such as reading textbooks, listening in class, taking essay tests, and writing reports—require them to think about and do. Without this knowledge of task requirements, they are unlikely to reach short-term and long-term academic goals.

Students' Knowledge About What Learning Strategies to Select and Use. Another type of knowledge that is important for successful learning is strategy knowledge. As noted earlier, strategies for studying and learning help students to orchestrate their cognitive resources, so that they can move things from the IPC into long-term memory more effectively and efficiently. Strategies help students select what to place on the conference table and what to take away when the conference is over.

Learning strategies include a wide variety of cognitive processes and behavioral skills. Weinstein and Mayer (1986) developed a taxonomy to describe major categories of strategies for studying and learning. Three categories of strategies are presented here, to highlight how different strategies for studying and learning lead to different levels of understanding and recall and may therefore be appropriate in different situations. These categories are *repetition strategies, elaboration strategies,* and *organization strategies.*

Repetition Strategies. Many instructional tasks require simple recall or identification of important information. Effective repetition strategies are found most frequently in introductory courses and training programs because the acquisition of basic knowledge is often a first step in the creation of a more extensive, integrated knowledge base in an area. For example, a basic repetition strategy for memorization is the use of flash cards. Repetition strategies are also useful when learning tasks involve knowledge and skills that extend beyond the superficial learning of lists or unrelated bits of information. Examples of more complex repetition strategies include highlighting class notes or copying key ideas from class readings (without elaborating on the information). Each of these activities helps the learner go over important information and creates further opportunities to improve learning and move the information into long-term memory. Generally speaking, repetition strategies are most appropriate in the early stages of building a base of knowledge in an area.

Elaboration Strategies. One of the ways we help move things from the IPC to long-term memory is by building bridges between what we already know and what we are trying to learn. With elaboration strategies, students build these bridges by using prior knowledge or experiences to make what they are trying to learn more meaningful and memorable. Examples of elaboration strategies include generating a mental image of a scene described in a novel, or relating a scientific principle to everyday experience. The more active the learner is in building connections between prior knowledge and new information, the more meaningful and thus the more memorable the new knowledge becomes. Types of elaboration strategies that require more active processing on the part of the student include paraphrasing, summarizing, applying a problem-solving strategy to a new problem, and creating analogies. For example, when we create an analogy between something we already know and something we are trying to learn, we compare and contrast, trying to use prior knowledge to help us make sense of the new material. The processes of comparing and contrasting help us to build connections to the new material, so that it is more easily moved into long-term memory.

Organization Strategies. Organization strategies require the translation or transformation of information into another form, and the creation of some sort of scheme to provide structure for this new form of the information. Here, too, the purpose is to help create added meaning for the information, so that it can move into long-term memory more effectively. It is easier to remember information that is structured in some way than it is to remember isolated bits without structure. Examples of basic organization strategies include grouping foreign-language vocabulary words by part of speech, or grouping the battles of World War II by geographical location. Complex tasks can often be made more meaningful and more manageable with organizational strategies, such as creating a hierarchy of main ideas to use in writing a term paper, generating a force diagram in physics, or creating an outline from class notes.

As with elaboration strategies, the facilitating effect of organization strategies is usually attributed both to the processing that is involved in creating the organization and to the product itself. When students come up with an organization or an elaboration, the mental activities that they engage in help them learn and remember the information.

Instructors' Cognitive Strategies for Teaching

It is not enough for students to know about the different strategies for studying and learning. They must also know how to use them and under what conditions it is appropriate to use them. Students must also want to use the strategies, believe they can use them successfully, and value the outcomes obtained. Facility with strategies comes from using a variety of them under different task conditions in a variety of subject areas. The instructional decisions and teaching methods that we select and implement profoundly affect students' knowledge about strategies and their use of them. By understanding how students use these strategies, instructors can become more alert to ways of fostering the development and use of strategies through course structures and activities.

Instructors' decisions about how to teach, like students' decisions about how to learn, are the products of prior knowledge and executive control (setting instructional goals, selecting plans of action for teaching course material, monitoring instruction during class, and evaluating the overall plan). Similarly, instructional strategies are most effective and efficient when instructors know about themselves as teachers, know about different instructional tasks, and know about different instructional strategies.

If the instructional goal is to help students learn course material in a meaningful way and move it along the memory continuum, then instructors' knowledge must have several components. *Self-knowledge* must include instructors' knowledge of themselves as instructors, as well as their knowledge of their students as learners. *Task knowledge* must include knowledge of the academic tasks appropriate for reaching desired instructional outcomes, as well as knowledge of how this interacts with students' task knowledge. *Strategy knowledge* must include not only instructional strategies for teaching content but also strategies for teaching students how to learn content (see Figure 1).

Instructors' Self-Knowledge and Knowledge of Students. College instructors need to know about their strengths and weaknesses as teachers,

Figure 1. Interrelationships Among Instructors' Self-Knowledge, Task Knowledge, and Strategy Knowledge

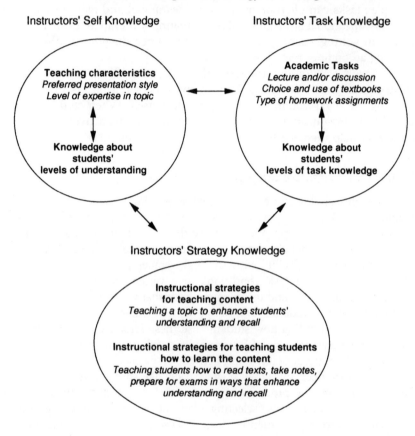

be aware of their preferences for certain teaching styles over others, and be conscious of their level of expertise in the courses they teach. For example, effective instructors are aware of the effects on students of how they present material, the way they evaluate students' work, and their choices of what subject matter to teach. Effective instructors are also aware of their students' strengths and weaknesses as learners and take these into account when developing or implementing instruction. Knowing about the similarities and differences between themselves and their students, in terms of prior knowledge, goals, motivation, and other variables, is critical for designing and implementing effective instruction.

Instructors' Knowledge About Task Characteristics. In addition to self-knowledge, task knowledge (such as about traditional requirements of a discipline) is reflected in such instructional decisions as how the course is organized (lecture, discussion, lab), the types of textbooks or other course materials to be used, and the format of examinations.

Other task characteristics that influence instructional strategies are the structure of the content domain and the goals of the course. All tasks occur within a particular content area and in a particular goals context. For example, some subject areas, like physics, have a fairly traditional order in which concepts are introduced. A course in modern literature, by contrast, may be extremely different each time it is offered, even though the same instructor teaches it. Furthermore, some courses are designed as prerequisites to others and have the goal of building a knowledge base, whereas other courses stand alone in that they are intended to give a general overview or awareness of an area. Each of these task characteristics influences instructional strategies.

The instructor must also be aware of the knowledge that students have about the content area and their understanding of the course structure, requirements, tasks, and goals. Do they know how to study from the textbook? Do they understand how to prepare for exams? Instructors must know about possible problems with students' prior knowledge or their misunderstandings about course requirements, so that these can be addressed and taken into account in teaching.

Instructors' Knowledge About Instructional and Learning Strategies. Many college instructors focus primarily on presenting course material. From the perspective of cognitive learning strategies, a focus on content may be necessary but not sufficient for optimal learning. Instructional plans should also include teaching students how to learn the content within the specific context of the course. Therefore, instructional strategies can be classified into two broad but complementary categories: strategies for communicating content effectively, and strategies for teaching students how to learn content.

Optimally, content instruction focuses on whether students are acquiring the information being presented, how they are integrating new ideas with prior knowledge, and to what extent they can use (recall, apply, transfer) the knowledge. Strategy instruction is motivated by similar outcomes, but the emphasis is on acquisition of strategy knowledge, orchestration of strategies, and acquisition of learning goals through strategy implementation and monitoring. By implementing an approach oriented toward cognitive learning strategies, the instructor focuses not only on what students are supposed to be learning but also on how they are learning. With this approach, remediation can be provided through additional content or help with learning how to learn about content.

Instructional Strategies for Teaching Course Content. Learning is a constructive process. Learning is like working an enormous jigsaw puzzle. The instructional challenge lies in the fact that every student has a one-of-a-kind puzzle, while instructors have the complete picture in their minds.

When information does not fit with what students already know, they may toss those pieces aside or take out their mental scissors and cut new pieces to fit their needs. Instruction, whether through lectures, class assignments, or labs, should help students develop knowledge (that is, help them recall prior knowledge and integrate it with new information), as well as help them use the knowledge to meet their goals for the course.

For instructional strategies to aid students in developing cohesive knowledge, the relationship between old knowledge and new information must be understood. Recalling prior knowledge is the first step in integrating new course concepts. For new information to be of later use, students must organize it within their prior knowledge or reorganize their prior knowledge around it. Otherwise, new information, if remembered at all, is recalled in isolated bits (as answers to particular questions in a specific course). There are some very clear limits to how many isolated bits of information we can recall, and those bits are subject to our forgetting. Therefore, the goal of instructional strategies for tapping prior knowledge is for students to increase their awareness of what they do not know and to define for themselves what they need to learn. This is part of the reason why many instructors give tests of prior knowledge at the beginning of their courses. This information helps instructors know more about the level and type of prior knowledge (or misconceptions) held by their students, and it helps students develop more awareness about their prior knowledge in relation to the course.

To further help students develop well-integrated knowledge, instructional strategies should aid students in checking their understanding of course material. Like practicing medicine, using instructional strategies to check students' understanding can be either preventive or diagnostic.

Examples of instructional strategies that help prevent misunderstanding are assigning work or providing for experiences in which students who have incorrect prior knowledge can confront their misconceptions, or requiring students to formally assess (via pretests, papers, exercises) their prior knowledge of content before beginning instruction. The basic assumption behind the preventive approach is that students may have errors in their prior knowledge (omissions, mistakes, incorrect associations) and that these problems must be addressed so that the new information is not incorporated into existing misconceptions.

Possible instructional strategies for diagnosing existing misunderstandings are asking students to talk aloud as they think through an answer, having students teach course topics or explain ideas to others, and reviewing students' notes, papers, or exams with them. Each of these methods is designed to help the instructor and students identify problems, so that they are solved before misunderstandings become a cohesive part of students' understanding.

Instructional Strategies for Teaching How to Learn. Because learning is a constructive process and instruction involves helping students integrate old and new knowledge appropriately, the optimal goal of any instructional strategy is to help students take more responsibility for their own learning and integration of knowledge. Instructing students in how to learn course content and monitor their own progress can put students in the driver's seat. However, like content instruction, strategy instruction not only includes helping students develop a repertoire of learning strategies but also involves helping them learn how to use these strategies effectively and efficiently in meeting goals. Students must learn about the strategies that are most appropriate for particular courses and why they are so useful (see Pressley, Borkowski, and Schneider, 1987, for a theoretical model of a good strategy user). It is not enough just to tell students about the strategies they should use in studying or trying to understand material; if students do not understand the benefits of particular strategies, they will be less motivated to use them on their own. Whether strategies are aimed at reading assigned texts, preparing for exams, or thinking like a historian, students need to know how to use the methods presented, but they must also value and want to use these methods if the methods are to be effective over time.

Knowing about different learning strategies and wanting to use them is not enough. Students need practice with a variety of learning strategies before they can understand when particular strategies are most effective or be helped to improve their efficiency in using the strategies. Instructors need to provide opportunities for students to practice using learning strategies. Students also need feedback about their strategy use and its effectiveness in different situations.

Conclusion

We have already compared learning with holding a conference; now we incorporate teaching into the picture. As instructors, we are also participants in the conference, but we participate from the head of the table. To ensure a successful conference, we encourage other participants to share the knowledge they bring with them, and we help them learn how to take as much material as possible away with them. As executive officers, we also have personal goals for the conference. We decide for ourselves what information to remember for the next meeting we call. We select strategies for remembering certain information and for getting other participants to remember it as well. We implement strategies and monitor their effectiveness and efficiency. We deal with any sources of problems during the meeting, and we evaluate our overall plan, to ensure future success. As executive officers, we manage the meeting so that the conference is successful, thus meeting our own goals. Participants meet conference goals, too, but they also learn how to process conference materials.

References

Anderson, J. R. *Cognitive Psychology and Its Implications*. San Francisco: Freeman, 1980.

Collins, A., and Smith, E. E. (eds.). *Readings in Cognitive Science: A Perspective from Psychology and Artificial Intelligence*. San Mateo, Calif.: Morgan Kaufman, 1988.

Gardner, H. *The Mind's New Science*. New York: Basic Books, 1985.

Knapp, T. J. "The Emergence of Cognitive Psychology in the Latter Half of the Twentieth Century." In T. J. Knapp and L. C. Robertson (eds.), *Approaches to Cognition: Contrasts and Controversies*. Hillsdale, N.J.: Erlbaum, 1986.

Mayer, R. E. *The Promise of Cognitive Psychology*. San Francisco: Freeman, 1981.

Pressley, M., Borkowski, J. G., and Schneider, W. "Cognitive Strategies: Good Strategy Users Coordinate Metacognition and Knowledge." *Annals of Child Development*, 1987, *4*, 89–129.

Weinstein, C. E., and Mayer, R. "The Teaching of Learning Strategies." In M. Wittrock (ed.), *The Handbook of Research on Teaching*. New York: Macmillan, 1986.

Claire E. Weinstein is professor in the Department of Educational Psychology, University of Texas, Austin.

Debra K. Meyer is assistant instructor in the Department of Educational Psychology, University of Texas, Austin.

*The precepts of cognitive psychology provide highly practical
suggestions for teachers and learners. These suggestions make
learning more efficient in the present and produce learners
who will be more self-sufficient in the future.*

Practical Implications of Cognitive Theories

Marilla D. Svinicki

To adopt cognitive theory is to build one's teaching practice on the following assertion:

> Learners are not simply passive recipients of information;
> they actively construct their own understanding.

The learner is at center stage. The instructor becomes a facilitator of learning, rather than one who delivers information. This perspective on learning
contrasts sharply with models that imply that learners get the point as long
as the instructor provides an appropriate stimulus. Cognitive psychology
says that the learner plays a critical role in determining what he or she gets
out of instruction.

As instructors, we may provide the same information to several students, but we cannot always predict how a student will interpret or use
the information. To illustrate this dilemma, consider what comes to mind
when you hear the word *cardinal*. Some individuals think of baseball,
some of numbers, some of the Roman Catholic church, some of the color
red. Some even think of sin; it all depends on background and current
mindset. As a teacher, my goal is that when I say the word *cardinal*,
everyone in the class makes the same association. It has been shown
(Naveh-Benjamin, McKeachie, Lin, and Tucker, 1986) that students who
make the same connections and use the same content-organization patterns as the instructor do best on standard measures of learning, no
matter how they start out organizing or associating content. This change
in the conception of what happens during learning makes big differences

in our perception of what students and teachers do in the classroom. Let us explore what some of those differences are.

Redefining the Student Role

Many students are under the impression that their task in class is passively to absorb what the teacher says in lecture, what is in the textbook, what they see in lab, and what they practice in homework. They are often unaware that what they think they absorb, read, see, or learn from practice may not be what the instructor intends. Their understanding of all these things is strongly influenced by a whole array of variables: their prior knowledge, their interpretation of what is important, the frequency with which they test themselves and their understanding, their perspectives on how all this relates to future use, and so on. Whether they realize it or not, and whether they like it or not, what they learn depends on who they are, where they have been, and what they do. Thus truth is no longer absolute; even the initial intake of information is subject to idiosyncratic interpretation. Scholars in the field of communication have long maintained that both the receiver and the medium are part of the message.

To be most effective, learners must become aware of how their own biases and behaviors filter the information they receive. They must also take a developmental step forward in their understanding of the epistemology of knowledge. They must come to understand that there are multiple ways of interpreting reality. In one cognitive-development model (Perry, 1981), this movement from a dualistic view of the world ("Truth is truth") to a multiplistic view ("Truth is subject to interpretation") carries with it a necessary change in one's view of oneself and in what one does during learning. It is the change from lower cognitive levels (memorization and simple translation of authoritative sources) to higher levels (analysis, evaluation, and acceptance of personal responsibility for one's choices).

Redefining the Instructor Role

For the instructor's role, the first implication of shifting to a cognitive perspective is that neither the teacher nor the content is at the center of the learning universe. Instructors become facilitators of learning. What we say is not necessarily what students get, unless we are very careful and deliberate about how it is presented. Information is easily garbled in transmission. Our job becomes one of minimizing the noise in the transmission, so that all the listeners (learners) interpret our statements in the same way, or in as close an approximation as possible, and store information in long-term memory so that they can retrieve it in the future. Better yet, we hope to convey the message in such a way that the learner can retrieve it without our intervention when the occasion demands. We do this by careful attention to how the content is structured, how it is sequenced, what examples and activities we use, how we respond to initial learning attempts, and an array of other instructional strategies.

A second implication for the instructor's role is that we are freed from our "Atlas complex" (Finkel and Monk, 1983). The weight of the world of learning does not rest on our shoulders alone; that responsibility is shared with students. They are the ones who must do the learning. They select the learning strategies, monitor their own comprehension, and chart their own future course. What we do is help them understand the tools they need for success and arrange the environment to make success possible.

These are difficult adjustments for teacher and student alike, but, in the end, students are better off. Someone will not always be there to decide for them what should and should not be learned, how to interpret new information, or what to believe. Those choices eventually fall to the learners. The college years are none too soon for learners to become self-sufficient.

Implications for Teaching

From the cognitive perspective, teachers are faced with two tasks. First, we must organize the course and its content in a way consistent with what we believe about how learning takes place, paying attention to structure, sequence, examples, and activities. Second, and simultaneously, we must help students learn how to learn content, a step in sophistication above the mere learning of content itself. Let us examine how these two tasks are translated into action. Here are six principles drawn from cognitive theory, along with some implications for teaching.

Principle 1. If information is to be learned, it must first be recognized as important. Implication: the more attention is effectively directed toward what is to be learned (that is, toward critical concepts and major areas), the higher the probability of learning.

It is easy to see this phenomenon in operation. Consider the way textbooks are structured. Important concepts are highlighted in bold or italic type. This draws the learner's eye immediately to those words, and they are interpreted as important. A lecturer does the same thing by writing a word on the board or putting up an overhead transparency. The lecturer can also highlight concepts by using an outline on the board, indicating the major components of the lecture. Verbal cues, such as "the next main point is . . . ," or vocal cues, such as slowing down perceptibly when emphasizing some idea, or repeating something important, can be used as highlighting. Phrasing an idea as a question is another way of drawing attention, by making it stand out from the background. In discussion classes, instructors draw attention to main ideas by writing them on the board, repeating them, incorporating them into a summary, or reacting favorably when they are raised by students.

Likewise, students need to learn to recognize the cues that help them identify what is important. This may be what students mean when they say they have learned to "psych out" the instructor. They learn to pick up cues, however subtle, that the instructor uses to denote the relative importance of material. Eventually, as students become more knowledgeable about the content itself, they can use that knowledge to help determine the importance of new information, without the need for external cues. As noted in the previous chapter, this is one of the differences between the ease of learning in an advanced course and in an introductory course. Without extensive background in a field, all content appears important, and students struggle to master everything. As they learn more, they develop a feeling for what is critical in the discipline. An instructor can do a lot to assist students in recognizing how the discipline determines what is important, by making such discriminations explicit in class. It cannot be accomplished in one class alone. Over the space of several classes, however, students can become more efficient in discriminating the critical features that make ideas important for a field.

Principle 2. During learning, learners act on information in ways that make it more meaningful. Implication: both instructor and student should use examples, images, elaborations, and connections to prior knowledge to increase the meaningfulness of information.

It is natural, in the flow of conversation, to cite examples, evoke images through metaphors and analogies, and translate abstractions into concrete instances for ease of understanding. Most instructors use these devices regularly in explaining content. All these devices depend heavily on students' prior knowledge and experience. An example does not clarify a concept if the student has no experience with that example. Saying that a *phratz* works just like a *klogue* does not help if you do not know how a *klogue* works in the first place. Thus it becomes important for an instructor to know students and their backgrounds and to use that knowledge in the selection of activities and examples for use in class.

Students should be encouraged to make their own connections between what is being studied in one class and what they have learned in previous classes or in other settings. For example, students can create personal bibliographies of texts and readings from other courses that are related to the content at hand and then use those materials to supplement assigned readings. Many instructors have students scan the news media for examples related to class concepts. Students can learn to use vivid images and other elaboration strategies, as described in the previous chapter, if the instructor allows time during class for such activities. Instructors can also counsel students to incorporate this practice of making content meaningful into their regular study procedures. An instructor who finds a student having difficulty creating class notes can suggest alternatives to make notes more meaningful. For example, class notes do not have to be exclusively in prose format; sketches and other visual stimuli can serve as helpful elaborations on a basic text. The common thread in these examples is to encourage students to make connections between what they know and what they are learning.

Principle 3. Learners store information in long-term memory in an organized fashion related to their existing understanding of the world. Implication: the instructor can facilitate the organization of new material by providing an organizational structure, particularly one with which students are familiar, or by encouraging students to create such structures; in fact, students learn best under the latter condition.

This principle is at the heart of the cognitive view of learning. We learn and remember information because we act on it in such a way as to fit it into an organized pattern based on our world view. Instructors who present course content in an organized fashion are increasing the probability that students will use that organizational structure to understand and store the content. For a single lecture, this means having a clear outline, displaying that outline as a guide to listening, and maintaining an orderly sequence of concepts and examples. Earlier, we saw that the outline enhances attention; here, we see it playing an additional role in learning.

In the overall course structure, organization means relating logical units of content to one another and building in a regular pattern toward the ultimate goal of the course. The pattern can be chronological, comparative, hierarchical, or representative of any other relationship. Whatever pattern is chosen, it should be made explicit to students.

The second part of the concept of organization is also important: relating the organizational structure to students' existing world views. In the absence of a clearly delineated structure from the instructor, students will impose on content the organization most closely related to their current view of things. Thus, in a history course, the organizational structure that students are most likely to choose is chronological; it is what they are used to and is often their sole view of how history is organized. If the instructor's thinking is organized around some other structure, such as causes and effects, and if that organization is not made clear to students, then class content may appear very confused and disorganized. In the sciences, the influence of students' preexisting organizations shows up in commonsense misconceptions about the causes of everyday phenomena. These misconceptions can create some bizarre attempts to explain events and are often very difficult to overcome.

In the absence of a preexisting organization or one provided by the instructor, students are likely to revert to rote memorization, a technique that may work in the short run but will eventually reach critical mass and produce failure. When new information is not or cannot be tied to old, students may easily encapsulate it as separate from everything else. This makes the new information hard to learn and easy to forget. It pays for the instructor to be aware of students' backgrounds and predispositions and to clarify which patterns of organizing the content are acceptable and which may be in conflict with those of the students.

Students can learn to recognize or create structures to facilitate their own learning. As noted earlier, one measure of students' grasp of content is the degree to which each student's conceptual map of the content organization matches the instructor's map. Getting in the habit of outlining readings and lecture notes, creating tree diagrams showing the relationships of concepts to one another, and learning other forms of content organization are tools students can use to make learning more efficient. By introducing students to these tools, an instructor helps them move closer to self-sufficiency.

Principle 4. Learners continually check understanding, which results in refinement and revision of what is retained. Implication: opportunities for checking and diagnosis aid learning.

Think about how you read different types of material. If you are truly attending to the material and not just skimming it, you constantly monitor your reading. Sometimes you are brought up short when you find a sentence that seems incongruent with your understanding of what has gone before. At that point, you back up and reread, to find the cause of the discrepancy. That practice illustrates comprehension monitoring, an important executive process in learning. In reading, we have the luxury of interrupting ourselves to check on understanding, going back and replaying what we have just read to look for inconsistencies. In classes, however, most students do not have that opportunity, because they are not in control of the pace of the class; the lecturer controls the pace. If they do not understand something or think they hear a discrepancy, few students have sufficient self-confidence to interrupt and ask for clarification. Their usual response is to write down verbatim what is being said and go back and check it later. Poorer students, especially, may have given up the monitoring process altogether, in favor of just getting it all down. They feel they do not have time to think during class.

The instructor could give them that time. Most instructors pause periodically and ask for questions. They may rarely hear the important questions, however, because they seldom wait long enough for students to formulate them. It takes a few seconds to mentally look back over what has just been said and check for understanding. It takes a few more seconds to create a question that will make sense to others and not make the questioner look foolish. That is already six seconds, at the minimum, and only for really good students who have been able to keep up. Most instructors have difficulty waiting even three seconds before moving on; no wonder we seldom get questions. Students do not understand everything perfectly—they are just not fast enough to recognize what they do not understand and then ask.

Once instructors become aware of the need for and difficulty of monitoring, they can take steps to help students engage in this important strategy. For example, as just discussed, learning to wait a little longer after inviting questions (known as *wait time*) can be a big help. An even more significant step is to be very directive about checking understanding. For example, many instructors insert pauses in their lectures, during which students are instructed to write a one- or two-sentence summary of what has just been discussed. One or two of these summaries are then reviewed out loud for accuracy. This practice gets students in the habit of thinking in terms of major ideas and summaries and periodically checking their understanding. Students who have not been able to produce the summaries become aware immediately that they did not understand something and can either ask questions or note their confusion for future questioning or remediation. This practice also provides the instructor with feedback on students' understanding before it is too late to do something about it. These are only a few examples of how monitoring can be built into a class. For additional ideas on monitoring, consult Cross and Angelo (1988).

Students can be encouraged to engage in their own comprehension monitoring. One particularly popular strategy is to set aside a column on each sheet of class notes. In this column, the student records monitoring questions as the lecture or class period proceeds, noting confusions, connections with other ideas, potential test questions, and so on. The mere presence of this column reminds the student to monitor thinking as the class proceeds.

Comprehension monitoring shows up most frequently in suggestions about reading. Students are encouraged to preview the reading and to record questions that they expect to be answered in the material. As they read, the need to answer those questions prompts students to process the reading at a deeper level than mere repetition of the words on the page. Getting in the habit of pausing at each break in the reading (say, where headings appear) and asking questions about what went before is another way of tracking comprehension. There are many possibilities for increasing awareness of understanding and its failure. Most important is to ensure that students see the need to pay attention to their attention.

Principle 5. Transfer of learning to new contexts is not automatic but results from exposure to multiple applications. Implication: provision must be made during initial learning for later transfer.

To believe that one exposure to material is sufficient to allow a student to use that information forever in the future is naïve. To believe that a beginning student is able to see all the potential uses for what he or she is learning is also naïve. Indeed, much of their schooling seems to have convinced students of the independence of content; what they learn in math class has no relationship to what they learn in English or chemistry, and vice versa. As instructors, however, we know that knowledge is interrelated and that using it in different contexts makes it more meaningful and more easily remembered. We also know that, in the real world, students are unlikely to encounter situations for using their new knowledge that are exactly the same as what they experience in the classroom. They must learn how to take what they learn and transfer it.

We can help them make that transfer by building it in from the very start. Our greatest tool for facilitating transfer is incorporating a wide range of application opportunities and settings into the learning situation. The more (and the more different) situations in which students see a concept applied, the better they will be able to use what they have learned in the future. It will no longer be tied to a single context.

An instructor can facilitate transfer through sheer repetition. The more we use a skill or concept, the more automatic its use becomes, until we hardly have to think about it at all. It is the rare student who can learn to solve a complex type of math problem after trying only one example. It takes many hours of practice to become proficient at most things, to reach a level of "automaticity." Why should intellectual skills be any different?

A final facilitator of transfer involves getting students to abstract the principle from the practice. If students can articulate the steps they are taking to solve problems, or if they can extract an underlying concept from a set of examples, then they will be more likely to use that abstraction in a different context. This is known as decontextualizing and is the more complex complement of "automaticity." In practice, an instructor can have students talk to one another about the processes they are going through to solve problems. In so doing, they become aware of the steps they use (Lochhead and Whimbey, 1987). This awareness is then translated into increased ability to apply the same steps, now detached from their original context, to a new situation.

Principle 6. Learning is facilitated when learners are aware of their learning strategies and monitor their use. Implication: the instructor should help students learn how to translate these strategies into action at appropriate points in their learning.

These six principles discuss instructors' activities in the context of teaching the content of specific courses, but they also apply to the content of knowing how to learn. (Learning strategies, too, can be viewed as content to be learned.) Attention should be drawn to learning strategies. Their use should be monitored, and their transfer to new settings should be ensured. When an instructor takes on the task of teaching both the content of the discipline and the content of learning strategies within the same course, he or she will enrich students in both areas. There are several objectives and instructional methods for teaching the content of learning strategies.

Students need to know what cognitive learning strategies are. Most students are not aware of the different strategies available to them. An instructor can illustrate the strategies that exist by taking every opportunity to point out the process of learning as it occurs. For example, to help students learn to recognize the cues that indicate the importance of material and the degree of attention it should receive, the instructor, during the first few class periods, can explain the purpose of using visuals or the blackboard to highlight important concepts, as well as how the textbook uses similar techniques to highlight important ideas. After the first lecture, the instructor can illustrate these strategies by taking a few minutes to show students how the organization of the lecture should be reflected in their notes and to remind them of how that organization was made explicit during the lecture itself. At the beginning of the next class period, students can be asked to recall the main points of the previous class and to discuss how the organizational structure helped them remember the main ideas. These are only a few examples of how an instructor can make learning strategies explicit in the context of the course itself. These strategies are applicable to listening in class, reading the textbook, preparing for exams, monitoring understanding, managing time, and a whole range of other general learning situations that students may never have analyzed in just this way.

Students need to know how to monitor their own use of learning strategies. Perhaps the best way an instructor can help students get in the habit of using learning strategies is by providing opportunities, within the structure of the course itself, for students to use them. As discussed earlier, the instructor can pause during class to allow students to monitor their comprehension, by asking questions of themselves and of the instructor. An instructor can incorporate an optional learning log, in which students keep track of ways they have applied some of the strategies suggested by the instructor. The instructor can build a component on time and resource management into a term paper assignment, so that students set up work schedules, with goals and action plans, early in the semester and monitor their adherence to or revision of those plans. The instructor can take time after an exam to work with students on understanding how to use errors to diagnose study problems. All these activities both give students the opportunity to use learning strategies in their classes and demonstrate how important the instructor thinks these strategies are.

Students need to know when to use the strategies they have learned. This is a more difficult task for the instructor, because much of the decision about when to use a strategy depends on students' individual needs, as well as on the context. Nevertheless, the instructor helps by providing information on what alternative strategies are available and how they can be applied to different situations. He or she can model different strategies while answering questions or solving problems raised in class. Too often, students believe that the instructor immediately knows all the answers to all questions asked; they do not realize that instructors frequently have to think through new problems and new questions, just as students do. Taking the opportunity to work on new problems with students and show how to approach a new situation serves as a good model for students to understand that different problems require different approaches.

Another opportunity to help students understand the situational contexts of learning strategies occurs when students come individually for assistance. Talking with them about the strategies they have tried, as well as working with them to develop new strategies for attacking new problems, can make them aware of the need to vary the solution with the situation.

Students need to know how to adapt their strategies to new situations. This is really the problem of transfer, taken one step farther. Just as we need to vary contexts in order for students to transfer content skills to new situations, we need to vary learning situations in order to show how strategies apply to different situations. Something that would be particularly helpful in this task is cooperation among instructors in different areas. This has been referred to as the *metacurriculum* (Weinstein, 1982): the idea of incorporating instruction in learning strategies into all courses, regardless of content. If instructors in chemistry used the same terms for learning strategies that instructors in history used, students would begin to decontextualize those strategies and then be more likely to apply them to French as well. They may not work identically in all fields, but many of the concepts can be applied across disciplines, or at least in similar contexts (for example, in all language classes or in all fact-based classes).

Summary

There is a great deal of intuitive appeal to the cognitive approach to teaching. It echoes our own experience as learners and is easy to understand. Applying the approach is more difficult, however, because we must give up our illusion of control. That change shakes the foundation of content as the primary focus of our teaching. We are then faced with the task of adapting to the needs of learners, a varied and unpredictable group. Fortunately, if we accept the precepts of cognitive theory—that learning is active, not passive—we will help to develop more productive learners who will function effectively and independently in the uncertainties of the future. Isn't that what it means to be a teacher?

References

Cross, K. P., and Angelo, T. *Classroom Assessment Techniques: A Handbook for Faculty.* Ann Arbor, Mich.: National Center for Research on Improving Postsecondary Teaching and Learning, 1988.

Finkel, D. L., and Monk, G. S. "Teachers and Learning Groups: Dissolving the Atlas Complex." In C. Bouton and R. Y. Garth (eds.), *Learning in Groups.* New Directions for Teaching and Learning, no. 14. San Francisco: Jossey-Bass, 1983.

Lochhead, J., and Whimbey, A. "Teaching Analytical Reasoning Through Thinking-Aloud Pair Problem Solving." In J. E. Stice (ed.), *Developing Critical Thinking and Problem-Solving Abilities*. New Directions for Teaching and Learning, no. 30. San Francisco: Jossey-Bass, 1987.

Naveh-Benjamin, M., McKeachie, W. J., Lin, Y.-G., and Tucker, D. G. "Inferring Students' Cognitive Structures and Their Development Using the 'Ordered Tree Technique.' " *Journal of Educational Psychology*, 1986, 78, 130–140.

Perry, W. G. "Growth in the Making of Meaning." In A. W. Chickering (ed.), *The Modern American College*. San Francisco: Jossey-Bass, 1981.

Weinstein, C. E. "A Metacurriculum for Remediating Learning-Strategies Deficits in Academically Underprepared Students." In L. Noel and R. Levitz (eds.), *How to Succeed with Academically Underprepared Students*. Iowa City, Iowa: American College Testing Service, National Center for Advancing Educational Practice, 1982.

Marilla D. Svinicki is director of the Center for Teaching Effectiveness, University of Texas, Austin.

*Theories of motivation suggest that appropriate attention to
students' needs and expectations for success will enhance
their involvement and learning.*

What Theories of Motivation Say
About Why Learners Learn

James H. McMillan, Donelson R. Forsyth

As college professors, we have often wondered why some students are
more involved in class, better prepared for discussions, ask more questions,
and, in general, simply try harder than other students with equal or better
ability. Why do some students learn more than others? Is it something
about them or us? More important, what can we do differently to enhance
learning? By trying to understand why students act as they do, we are
struggling with what psychologists and educators term *motivation*—a some-
what mysterious dispositional quality that facilitates learning. This construct
has played a key role in researchers' attempts to understand all forms of
learning. In this chapter, we will concentrate on recent theories of motivation that have particular relevance for college teaching and learning. In the
following chapter, we will summarize practical implications of the theories
for improving teaching and learning. More detailed perspectives on theories
of motivation can be found in Ames and Ames (1984, 1985, 1989), and
Weiner (1980).

What Is Motivation?

Motivation is defined in a general way by educators and psychologists as
the processes that initiate and sustain behavior. Motivation can be defined
more specifically for learning in college courses as purposeful engagement
in classroom tasks and study, to master concepts or skills. It is not simply a
matter of performing a task, getting a good grade, or accumulating units for
graduation. We believe, as suggested by Ames (1990) and Brophy (1983),
that motivation is a process in which students value learning and involve

NEW DIRECTIONS FOR TEACHING AND LEARNING, no. 45, Spring 1991 ©Jossey-Bass Inc., Publishers themselves in classroom assignments and activities. Motivated students, from our perspective, take learning seriously and try to get maximum benefits, rather than merely getting by or doing the minimum amount of work necessary. The question is "What do current theories of motivation offer to college professors who want to enhance the purposeful engagement of their students?" Before we answer this question, some assumptions need to be clarified, so that we can effectively apply the theories to practice.

First, students can be motivated to greater involvement and higher achievement. Theoretical perspectives have been translated into applied research to show that appropriate instructional behaviors and course structures will enhance students' motivation.

Second, motivation concerns three fundamental questions: What originates or initiates students' arousal or activity? What causes a student to move toward a goal? What causes a student to persist in striving toward a goal? Theories of motivation may be concerned with one or all three questions. Early research in motivation emphasized the first question, seeking to identify biological influences, such as physiological deficits, instincts, appetite, and chemical controls. Much of the research was conducted in laboratories, with rats and other animals, to see what moved a resting organism to activity (Weiner, 1990). These theories, along with others, such as psychoanalytical theory and Hullian theory, emphasize innate needs that seem far removed from the college classroom.

Third, motivational theories tend to emphasize factors within individuals or factors in the environment. Factors within individuals are traits that students bring to the classroom, such as fear of failure and its accompanying anxiety or the strong need to achieve high grades and get into graduate school. Other theories are concerned with environmental factors, such as the manner in which lectures are given, the competitiveness of the grading system, or the rapport the instructor establishes with students.

Fourth, while questions concerning motivation are simple, the answers are complex, involving a multitude of factors in both the students and the environment. Consequently, no one theory or perspective can be applied to every situation. Each one is insufficient by itself, and thus many theories must be considered simultaneously, in order to take action that will increase students' involvement in learning. (The model of motivation that we have developed is a heuristic one that helps organize these theories.)

Fifth, most theories of classroom motivation focus on needs or cognitions of students. Needs are deficiencies within students but can be influenced significantly from external sources. Cognitive theories, which maintain that thoughts and mental processes are crucial in determining motivation, currently dominate the motivational literature. (Significant need- and cognitive-based theories will be summarized in the context of the model.)

A Heuristic Model of Motivation

On the basis of social learning theory (Rotter, 1966), the expectancy theories of Atkinson (1964) and Vroom (1964), and earlier work by McMillan (1980), we have developed a model to organize what we believe are, theoretically, the most important influences of motivation for learning (see Figure 1).

The model is based on the premises that academic learning is primarily a cognitive activity and that students' motivation is heavily influenced by their thinking about what they perceive as important and what they believe they can accomplish. According to this model, two crucial categories of factors determine motivation: needs and expectations. Needs, which have dominated much of the earlier literature on motivation, initiate action to satisfy them. The term *expectations* refers to the student's belief about the probability that a need will be met as the result of a particular behavior. Simply stated, motivation is a function of both needs and expectations. If

Figure 1. A Heuristic Model of College Students' Motivation

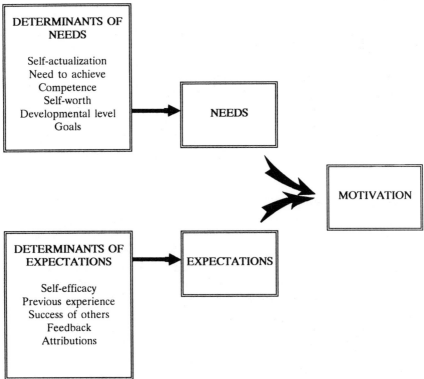

needs are present, and if students believe they are able to satisfy the needs, then they will be motivated to behave in ways that will meet the needs. If students perceive that there is little chance for high achievement and that it is not important to do well, then they will not be motivated to learn. Both needs and expectations are necessary because it is unlikely for students to be motivated at all if there is either no need or no expectation for success.

What factors influence the motivational strength of any given need? This model, taking a cognitive behavioral approach (Rotter, 1966; Bandura, 1977), stresses the value of meeting the need. Rotter (1966), for example, argues that "reinforcement value" combines with expectancies to determine achievement behavior. Reinforcement value is the importance or preference given to the probable result of the behavior. For instance, high achievement in one's major may have greater value than high achievement in electives, suggesting greater motivation to learn in major courses. Rotter integrates reinforcement value with needs, postulating that behaviors will have greater value if they satisfy needs, such as recognition or status, dominance, independence, protection or dependency, and love or affection (Rotter and Hochreich, 1975). Another approach is to think of any task or outcome as having some degree of value. Subjective task value has three components (Eccles and Wigfield, 1985): attainment value (the importance of success to meet needs, such as self-esteem or competence), intrinsic value (the extent to which the task is inherently interesting or enjoyable), and utility value (the importance of success for attaining long-range goals). These components are represented as different determinants of needs in our model.

In the remainder of this chapter, we summarize theories of motivation, to show how particular determinants of needs and expectations affect choices of behavior, level of involvement, and persistence. In the next chapter, we consider the practical implications of the model.

Needs

Needs tend to motivate students to behave so as to attain satisfaction and rewards. They are innate feelings and beliefs that direct attention and energy toward determining priorities and goals, which in turn influence the level of engagement in learning. With college students, there are important determinants of needs that help us understand their motives.

Several well-established theories emphasize different kinds of needs. Those that have the most relevance to college students' learning are summarized here. Other needs, like the physiological needs for food, sleep, and water, and psychoanalytical theories that stress unconscious processes and defense mechanisms are not included.

Self-Actualization. Actualization theorists argue that human beings constantly strive to maximize their human potential—that we seek to be as competent, creative, and effective as possible. Often the terms *self-actual-ization* and *fulfillment* are used to describe this need. The theories empha-size that persons are motivated to act in ways that will most enhance self-actualization and fulfillment.

Rogers (1961) maintains that progress toward personal fulfillment is the single and primary source of motivation. He uses the term *actualizing tendency* to describe this motive and believes that enhancement is defined uniquely for each individual. It is what is meaningful from the perspective of the student, for example, that is important, not what the professor thinks should be fulfilling. Because students are motivated by what they believe will move them toward what they believe will enhance self-actualization, motivation varies from one student to another. For one student, maximizing potential may mean high achievement in a course; for another, it may mean social approval. Developmental theories, as will be pointed out, provide some general guidelines for how college students define full realization of potential and self-actualization.

Rogers also emphasizes the needs of positive regard from others and positive self-regard. The need for positive regard from others is met as the individual attains acceptance from others. Acceptance is perceived as oth-ers relate in a manner that shows the positive value and worth of the person. Self-regard concerns the need for self-approval, the need to be satisfied with one's perceptions of oneself. According to Rogers, positive regard from others is necessary for self-regard; thus fulfillment is highly dependent on one's social environment and interpersonal relationships. With respect to college students, this suggests that as professors offer approval and support for what students see as important for their self-actualization, their motivation will be enhanced. If assignments, discus-sions, and out-of-class interactions are related to ideas, topics, and themes connected with personal fulfillment, students will be more likely to be motivated to learn. Even when the content of a course is difficult to relate to what is actualizing for students, positive regard from the professor will probably increase motivation to learn.

Self-actualization is at the top of Maslow's (1954) well-known hierar-chy of needs. At the bottom of the hierarchy are physiological and safety needs, which must be met before a person will be motivated to satisfy belonging, love, and esteem needs. These in turn must be satisfied before self-actualization. A higher need generally emerges only after lower needs have been met; thus students may be ideally motivated for achievement when love and belonging needs (such as for friendship and acceptance of others) have been met. Maslow's hierarchy suggests that classes in which students have positive regard for one another and feel a sense of caring from the professor will be more motivated to be creative and achieve.

Need to Achieve. One of the most fully developed and relevant need models for teaching and learning is achievement motivation theory (Atkinson and Feather, 1966; McClelland, 1961). This theory is based on the premise that a stable personality characteristic, termed the *need to achieve,* is an important determinant of achievement-related behaviors in any learning situation. Depending on childhood environment (especially parenting) and other experiences, some people develop a strong need to achieve success, while others develop a need to avoid failure. Individuals with a strong need to achieve success strive for excellence and are motivated by a sense of accomplishment and pride in achievement, not by rewards. They possess an intrinsic desire not only to do well but also to invest themselves independently in learning. They tend to be motivated by tasks with moderate risks of success or failure, and they perceive failure as feedback necessary for improving their performance. Persons with a strong need to avoid failure are not naturally drawn to achievement situations, especially if there is a chance of failure. These individuals have learned that failure is bad and leads to shame and humiliation. Rather than pursuing tasks with moderate risks, they prefer tasks that are either so easy that success is certain or so hard that success is impossible. In some cases, any feeling of failure is avoided by overachieving: trying too hard, and never being content with anything but top-notch performance (Covington and Beery, 1976).

Students with a high need for achievement will be attracted to challenging and moderately difficult learning tasks. Students with a need to avoid failure may exhibit anxiety and fear. They will need more structure and more positive feedback.

Competence. A primary need motive for most college students is to become competent—to affect one's environment. This need involves achieving mastery and accomplishment, feeling a sense of control. Individuals tend to seek out situations in which such feelings of competence are possible. Deci (1975) suggests that students seek out stimulation and challenges in order to feel competent, and that, by resolving moderately discrepant inputs and inconsistency, students fulfill a need for self-determination. Chickering (1969, 1981) points out that the development of competence is a primary growth area of college students. Students are in need of experiences that build their confidence in their ability to handle college-level work. They need opportunities to engage in meaningful intellectual tasks, and they need specific feedback in order to know they have been successful.

Self-Worth. A fundamental need that pervades achievement situations is for individuals to maintain a positive view of themselves. Covington (1984) and Covington and Beery (1976) theorize that much of students' behavior is designed to enhance their self-worth. Self-worth needs affect both the choice to be involved in achievement situations and interpretations of performance that affect subsequent motivation. In competitive situations, two conditions affect behavior to enhance self-worth— scarcity of rewards, and the tendency to equate the ability to achieve with self-worth. The emphasis on ability, which is prevalent among college students, coupled with grading on the curve and other competitive practices, tends to promote the notion that grades are evidence of ability; that is, when one student out of a class of thirty receives an A, that achievement suggests strong ability. Conversely, students who fail may interpret their achievement as an indication of low ability, particularly if high effort was exerted. When students believe that an upcoming situation holds little hope for obtaining scarce rewards, behaviors are adopted to avoid the feelings of negative self-worth that would accompany low achievement. Such students may be motivated to avoid failure or the implications of failure. Strategies are employed to shift the causes of failure away from personal ability and toward factors beyond individual control or responsibility. In this way, poor achievement is blamed on things other than ability, which in turn protects (or at least does not damage) self-worth. Thus students may be motivated to engage in such behaviors as not trying or procrastination. They may wait until the last minute to study for tests: if they fail, little information about their ability is communicated; if they succeed, it must be because they have high ability. Other behaviors include doing as little as possible, absenteeism, inattention, and cheating. All are contrary to what has been suggested as desirable—to be involved and try as much as possible. While some failure-avoiding behavior is related to fear of failure (achievement motivation), classes that offer sufficient rewards and encourage an emphasis on effort, rather than on ability, increase task involvement (Covington, 1984).

Developmental Level. College students are motivated by what interests them, what challenges them, and what competencies or abilities they feel a need to improve. During the past three decades, a number of developmental theories of college students have been articulated that help us understand where students are and how students change during college (Knefelkamp, Widick, and Parker, 1978). These theories are not motivational per se, but they do identify sequences, or stages—systematic changes over time, which elucidate concerns, goals, and areas of need. To illustrate the contribution of developmental principles to motivation, we will focus on two well-known theories: Chickering's model of student development, and Perry's theory of intellectual and ethical development.

Chickering (1969, 1981) has postulated a psychosocial model in which traditional-age college students have particular developmental tasks or concerns. He refers to seven "vectors" of development to categorize these tasks: developing competence, managing emotions, developing autonomy, establishing identity, freeing interpersonal relationships, developing purpose, and developing integrity. These vectors represent primary areas of concerns, or needs, for students. For example, development of autonomy involves independence from one's parents, gradually looking to peers for cues to know how to act in various situations, and finally relying more on one's own thoughts and values. Autonomy also involves recognition of interdependence with others, to balance the constant concern to establish identity. Developing integrity involves defining a set of values.

The more students can be engaged in these issues, the more likely they are to be motivated. Chickering believes that in each area students need to be challenged and stimulated, to encourage new behaviors and thinking. Students who do not experience analytical and critical thinking in classrooms are unlikely to feel competent as adult problem solvers. To foster developmental change and thus promote motivation, Chickering recommends environments that engage students in choices, diversity of interactions, direct and diverse experiences, and complex contemporary problems and that provide feedback and self-evaluation (Widick, Parker, and Knefelkamp, 1978).

Perry's scheme of intellectual and ethical development provides a basis for understanding how students think about and take responsibility for what they know, believe, and value (Perry, 1970). From the motivational standpoint, students are most likely to be engaged and interested when they are challenged by thinking that is beyond their current viewpoints. Students who use dualistic thinking—in which knowledge and the world exist in absolute categories, "rights" and "wrongs"—will be challenged by professors who introduce multiplicity and relativism, showing students that there are multiple perspectives on problems and that authorities may be wrong. Similarly, relativistic students who are challenged by their instructors' commitment to certain basic ideas will be motivated to move from relativism toward commitment (King, 1978). Students will be least likely to be motivated by the classroom activities, assignments, and discussions that are consistent with their current positions.

Goals. Students' needs are also determined by the goals they set for themselves. Goals can be short-term, such as a goal to achieve a certain grade on a test, or long-term, involving career decisions. We have already seen how one's need for achievement can affect goals—those with a high need for success select goals demonstrating excellence and tend to be most motivated when there is feedback of results and some risk of failing (Atkinson, 1964). Thus there is a preference for moderately difficult yet reachable, meaningful goals (Deci, 1975). The challenge for us is to know when students perceive goals (assignments, tests) as moderately difficult. Clearly, according to this theory, students in easy classes are unlikely to be motivated. It is also important to select goals and objectives that are worth learning. Often, to increase students' perceptions of task value, we need to explicitly indicate why learning is worthwhile. When we set goals and make a commitment to reaching them, motivation is increased (Bandura and Schunk, 1981). It has also been demonstrated that when students focus on learning goals (concerned with increasing their competence) rather than on performance goals (concerned with favorable evaluations of competence), they are more likely to select challenging tasks, with the intent to acquire new skills and competencies (Dweck and Leggett, 1988).

Expectations

It is well established that students' evaluations of their ability to achieve will influence their level of effort in learning. Students need to believe that, with reasonable effort, they can perform a task successfully. The determinants of expectations emphasize cognitive theories of motivation.

Self-Efficacy. Perceived self-efficacy involves beliefs about abilities to perform behaviors to attain designated outcomes (Bandura, 1986). Students with high self-efficacy have high expectations and are more likely to engage in learning. Students with low self-efficacy have low expectations and are likely to avoid efforts to learn. High self-efficacy is especially important in difficult learning tasks, since students who believe they are capable of performing well tend to persist longer than students who doubt their abilities (Schunk, 1990). Self-efficacy influences choice of activities and emotional reactions. Students tend to choose tasks that are consistent with self-appraisals of ability or probability of success and do so with reduced fear and anxiety. Students who are confident that they can successfully complete tasks are also more likely to engage in complex learning, such as problem solving (Bandura, 1986). Self-efficacy is enhanced as students make meaningful progress toward mastery and competence in a way that clearly implies that they are responsible for their success. Thus good performance is not necessarily an indication of increasing self-efficacy. Students need to realize that they have increased their competence through their own efforts. A key concept here is students' self-perceptions. Students are guided most by how they see themselves, not by other, objective evidence. Thus it is best to check out with students, on a personal basis, their feelings of self-efficacy.

Previous Experience. Students who have previously performed well in particular content areas or on particular learning tasks are likely to have high expectations of being able to perform well in similar areas or tasks. Likewise, a history of difficulty or failure will produce negative expectations. Thus, content and tasks that are familiar to students who have achieved meaningful success will lead to high expectations, while expectations for students who have had difficulty in the past can be enhanced by stressing that the content and learning tasks are new.

Success of Others. Self-evaluations and expectations are influenced by social comparisons, especially where objective standards of performance are lacking. Even in classrooms that utilize criterion-referenced goals, students, by observing the success of others, tend to come to certain conclusions to explain their performance. If all others are equally successful, then expectations may be positive in the future only if the situation is the same. Attribution theory, as we shall see, shows how such comparison cues are translated into expectations.

Feedback. Expectations can be influenced greatly by feedback from professors. If a source is credible and trustworthy, positive feedback about abilities is likely to lead to increased expectations and motivation. Similarly, students tend to discount feedback from less credible or less trustworthy professors. Students also tend to disregard feedback from professors who do not seem to understand students' abilities, task demands, or contextual factors. It is well documented that teachers' expectations can influence students' expectations, and feedback is a primary means of communicating teachers' expectations. Feedback is most helpful when it is specific and immediate. Feedback about performance is generally more motivating than simple rewards or reinforcements, because the information is meaningful to the student. If you reward students extrinsically with grades, to bribe them into performance, it is possible to decrease their motivation for continuing the behavior in the future (Deci, 1975). Students' attention should be on learning and on their competence, not on achieving rewards.

Attributions. Attribution theorists, concerned with explanations and justifications for success and failure, contribute to our understanding of both needs and expectations. Students explain their successes and failures in many ways. For example, some students attribute what they perceive to be success to their high ability and effort; others attribute failure to bad luck, unfair tests, or lack of sleep the night before. These attributional factors have been characterized along three dimensions identifying five causal distinctions (Weiner, 1984): (1) locus; (2) constancy, including temporal stability and globality; and (3) responsibility, including controllability and intentionality. *Locus* refers to whether the cause is contingent on something within the individual (internal), such as ability or effort, or on an external factor, such as test difficulty or the grading procedure. *Constancy* refers to the duration of the attribution, whether stable or unstable, global or situation-specific. *Responsibility* refers to whether the cause is controlled and/or intentional.

The nature of students' attributions affects their subsequent expectations because of the consequences of certain beliefs (Forsyth, 1986; Weiner, 1984):

1. Success attributed to such internal, stable factors as high ability results in higher future expectations.
2. Failure attributed to such external, unstable factors as luck results in lower future expectations.
3. Success attributed to external factors that are not expected to continue results in lower expectations.
4. Failure attributed to such internal, unstable, controllable factors as effort leads to higher expectations.
5. Failure attributed to such internal, stable factors as low ability results in lower expectations.

Attribution theory has also shown that beliefs about causes of success and failure influence emotional reactions, which in turn affect behavior

(Weiner, 1984). The most important determinant of emotion is the outcome—the student's perception of success or failure. There are positive, good feelings with success and negative feelings with failure. There are also more specific affects associated with particular attributions:

1. Success attributed to help from others results in gratitude.
2. Failure attributed to internal, controllable factors results in guilt.
3. Failure attributed to stable factors results in hopelessness.
4. Success attributed to internal, controllable factors results in pride and happiness.

It is not hard to understand how emotions affect motivation. Students who feel sad, helpless, fearful, or guilty will act very differently from students who feel happy, confident, and self-assured. The attributional theory of motivation can be summarized as follows:

achievement → antecedents → attributions → expectancies, → motivation
  behavior   to attributions   affect

After success or failure (*achievement behavior*), students incorporate information that can be thought of as *antecedents* in order to make *attributions,* which in turn determine *expectancies* and *affect.* The first and most important antecedent is the individual's initial expectations for how well he or she will do. Expected outcomes are likely to result in stable attributions, while unexpected outcomes lead to unstable attributions. Students who expect success and who are successful tend to attribute their performance to ability. If they fail, they attribute the outcome to factors that are consistent with high ability, such as lack of effort or unfair testing. Another antecedent is knowing how many other students succeeded or failed, which is readily available information if the instructor makes grade distributions public. If the majority of students succeed, an individual is likely to attribute success to an external cause, such as an easy test, while students who fail will attribute failure to internal factors. Thus, when one's outcome is the same as everyone else's, the attribution is external; when it is different, the attribution is internal. This attributional tendency suggests that when most students in a class succeed, professors need to emphasize that the performance was unlike that of many other classes and was due to internal causes.

Effort is also an important antecedent. If students exert a great deal of effort and fail, the tendency is to find external causes or attribute failure to lack of ability. Brophy (1983) points out that motivation is higher when students succeed with reasonable rather than with high effort, so that they see themselves as capable. This suggests that professors can help students understand what constitutes reasonable effort, and that both ability and effort are important for motivation. Clearly, students should not be expected to succeed only when they exert maximum effort.

Summary

Students are motivated to the extent that they initiate and sustain meaningful involvement in learning. Our model of motivation suggests that two factors—needs and expectations—are primary influences of motivation. Unfortunately, not much research has integrated the various theories of motivation that suggest determinants of needs and expectations. We can conclude, however, that students are likely to be motivated if their needs are being met, if they see value in what they are learning, and if they believe that they are able to succeed with reasonable effort. When all three of these factors are high, motivation will also be high. If students see little value in what they are learning or in the results of their effort, their motivation to be meaningfully engaged will be lessened, even if they believe that they are capable of success. We have been able to touch on only a few of the theories that are most relevant to college students' learning, but the research does provide a basis for professors' behavior, classroom activities, grading, and feedback to students that will enhance motivation by increasing perceived value, to better meet needs and build positive expectations for success.

References

Ames, C. A. "Motivation: What Teachers Need to Know." *Teachers College Record,* 1990, *91,* 409–421.

Ames, C., and Ames, R. (eds.). *Research on Motivation in Education.* Vol. 2. *The Classroom Milieu.* Orlando, Fla.: Academic Press, 1985.

Ames, C., and Ames, R. (eds.). *Research on Motivation in Education.* Vol. 3. *Goals and Cognitions.* Orlando, Fla.: Academic Press, 1989.

Ames, R., and Ames, C. (eds.). *Research on Motivation in Education.* Vol. 1. *Student Motivation.* Orlando, Fla.: Academic Press, 1984.

Atkinson, J. W. *An Introduction to Motivation.* Princeton, N.J.: Van Nostrand, 1964.

Atkinson, J. W., and Feather, N. T. *A Theory of Achievement Motivation.* New York: Wiley, 1966.

Bandura, A. *Social Learning Theory.* Englewood Cliffs, N.J.: Prentice-Hall, 1977.

Bandura, A. *Social Foundations of Thought and Action: A Social-Cognitive Theory.* Englewood Cliffs, N.J.: Prentice-Hall, 1986.

Bandura, A., and Schunk, D. H. "Cultivating Competence, Self-Efficacy, and Intrinsic Interest Through Proximal Self-Motivation." *Journal of Personality and Social Psychology,* 1981, *41,* 586–598.

Brophy, J. "Conceptualizing Student Motivation." *Educational Psychologist,* 1983, *18,* 200–215.

Chickering, A. W. *Education and Identity.* San Francisco: Jossey-Bass, 1969.

Chickering, A. W., and Associates. *The Modern American College: Responding to the New Realities of Diverse Students and a Changing Society.* San Francisco: Jossey-Bass, 1981.

Covington, M. V. "The Motive for Self-Worth." In R. Ames and C. Ames (eds.), *Research on Motivation in Education*. Vol. 1. *Student Motivation*. Orlando, Fla.: Academic Press, 1984.

Covington, M. V., and Beery, R. *Self-Worth and School Learning*. New York: Holt, Rinehart & Winston, 1976.

Deci, E. L. *Intrinsic Motivation*. New York: Plenum Press, 1975.

Dweck, S. S., and Leggett, E. L. "A Social-Cognitive Approach to Motivation and Personality." *Psychological Review*, 1988, *95,* 256–273.

Eccles, J., and Wigfield, A. "Teacher Expectations and Student Motivation." In J. B. Dusek (ed.), *Teacher Expectancies*. Hillsdale, N.J.: Erlbaum, 1985.

Forsyth, D. R. "An Attributional Analysis of Students' Reactions to Success and Failure." In R. S. Feldman (ed.), *The Social Psychology of Education*. New York: Cambridge University Press, 1986.

King, P. M. "William Perry's Theory of Intellectual and Ethical Development." In L. Knefelkamp, C. Widick, and C. A. Parker (eds.), *Applying New Developmental Findings*. New Directions for Student Services, no. 4. San Francisco: Jossey-Bass, 1978.

Knefelkamp, L., Widick, C., and Parker, C. A. (eds.). *Applying New Developmental Findings*. New Directions for Student Services, no. 4. San Francisco: Jossey-Bass, 1978.

McClelland, D. C. *The Achieving Society*. Princeton, N.J.: Van Nostrand, 1961.

McMillan, J. H. "Social Psychology and Learning." In J. H. McMillan (ed.), *The Social Psychology of Learning*. Orlando, Fla.: Academic Press, 1980.

Maslow, A. *Motivation and Learning*. New York: Harper & Row, 1954.

Perry, W. G., Jr. *Forms of Intellectual and Ethical Development in the College Years*. New York: Holt, Rinehart & Winston, 1970.

Rogers, C. R. *On Becoming a Person*. Boston: Houghton Mifflin, 1961.

Rotter, J. B. "Generalized Expectancies for Internal Versus External Control of Reinforcement." *Psychological Monographs,* 1966, *80* (entire issue 1).

Rotter, J. B., and Hochreich, D. J. *Personality*. Glenview, Ill.: Scott, Foresman, 1975.

Schunk, D. H. "Perceptions of Efficacy and Classroom Motivation." Paper presented at the annual meeting of the American Educational Research Association, Boston, 1990.

Vroom, V. H. *Work and Motivation*. New York: Wiley, 1964.

Weiner, B. *Human Motivation*. New York: Holt, Rinehart & Winston, 1980.

Weiner, B. "Principles for a Theory of Student Motivation and Their Application Within an Attributional Framework." In R. Ames and C. Ames (eds.), *Research on Motivation in Education*. Vol. 1. *Student Motivation*. Orlando, Fla.: Academic Press, 1984.

Weiner, B. "History of Motivational Research in Education." *Journal of Educational Psychology,* 1990, *82,* 616–622.

Widick, P., Parker, C. A., and Knefelkamp, L. "Arthur Chickering's Vectors of Development." In L. Knefelkamp, C. Widick, and C. A. Parker (eds.), *Applying New Developmental Findings*. New Directions for Student Services, no. 4. San Francisco: Jossey-Bass, 1978.

James H. McMillan is associate professor of educational studies at Virginia Commonwealth University. His interests include motivation and learning of college students and assessment of educational outcomes.

Donelson R. Forsyth is director of undergraduate studies and professor in the Department of Psychology, Virginia Commonwealth University. He is currently researching the attributional and emotional consequences of students' reactions to their academic successes and failures.

Three prescriptions offered by theories of motivation—reshape students' overall achievement orientation, create an expectation for success, and increase the specificity and value of academic outcomes—offer practical suggestions for enhancing learning.

Practical Proposals for Motivating Students

Donelson R. Forsyth, James H. McMillan

Motivation is an irrelevancy to some college educators. Laborers may need to be properly motivated by their supervisors, football players may require pumping up before the big game, and listless high school students may need to be seduced into the excitement of learning—but college students? Aren't they supposed to be self-motivated?

Certainly some students come to the classroom ready to expend considerable time and effort in their quest to learn the course material and achieve personal goals of success. Yet, for many students, the motivational pump is unprimed. Students' degree programs often require certain courses, so students may not be interested in the material, since they did not choose the course themselves, or perhaps they consider its content irrelevant to their personal goals. The course may be so challenging or so easy that discouragement or disillusionment may set in. Students also have jobs and other life pursuits to contend with, and these extracurricular activities may be far more exciting or involving than the act of learning.

Given that self-motivated learners exist only rarely in the college classroom, what can teachers do to increase their students' motivation to learn? This chapter, by building on the theoretical analyses presented in the previous chapter, focuses on needs, expectations, and goals. We first consider how one particularly important need—achievement orientation—influences motivation, by examining ways of restructuring this orientation if it is not conducive to learning. Next, because even the most motivated students will not strive to achieve when they are certain that failure is inevitable, we examine ways to create the expectation of success. Last, we turn to ways to increase the value of academic outcomes, by helping stu-

NEW DIRECTIONS FOR TEACHING AND LEARNING, no. 45, Spring 1991 ©Jossey-Bass Inc., Publishers

dents develop personal goals and identify the means of achieving these goals. Throughout, our focus is on methods that classroom instructors can use to modify these three determinants of motivation.

Need to Achieve

As noted in the preceding chapter, theorists have conceptualized learners' need to achieve in a variety of ways. To some, the key difference between high and low achievers is self-esteem: low achievers lack self-confidence and consider themselves failures (Purkey, 1970). Others, by contrast, emphasize individual variations in locus of control (Rotter, 1966), self-efficacy (Bandura, 1977), need for achievement (McClelland, 1985), competence motivation (White, 1959), self-control (Carver and Scheier, 1981), personal causation (deCharms, 1976, 1987), and intrinsic motivation (Deci and Ryan, 1985). These variations, however, need not be considered unalterable. Whereas early personality theorists felt that achievement orientation was a stable trait that remained constant across situations and was not easily altered, an interactional view assumes that one's general need to achieve interacts with features of the setting, to determine overall achievement motivation. A student who is unmotivated in one situation may become the epitome of the hard-striving, goal-oriented student in another. The key is to take care in structuring the classroom situation, so that motivation is gained rather than lost.

Capitalize on Intrinsic Motivation. The desire to learn—to discover, to comprehend, to synthesize, to develop—is an intrinsic part of human nature, and this intrinsic motivation to learn should be exploited. Although educators too frequently assume that students are reluctant learners, in many cases they become reluctant only after their initial intrinsic motivation is wiped away by hours of uninspired lectures in which instructors convey their own contempt for the subject matter. Instructors should do all they can to capitalize on intrinsic motivation, by taking certain simple steps (Ames, 1987; Brophy, 1987; Condry, 1987; Deci and Ryan, 1985; Lepper, 1983).

Introduce the course and each topic in an interesting, informative, and challenging way. You should not just review the syllabus during the first session or concentrate on how grades will be determined. Instead, you should highlight the stimulating intellectual tasks to be accomplished, pique students' curiosity, challenge traditional views, and hint at inconsistencies to be resolved.

Present material at a challenging level that communicates respect for your students and their abilities. Monitor the pace at which you present ideas, so that you maintain a balance between a slow pace that leads to boredom and a too-fast pace that leads to confusion.

Use varied and creative styles of teaching to avoid monotony and keep students' interest high. You should be unpredictable but not capricious. Introduce odd but provocative ideas, take the role of devil's advocate, and let students participate in the classroom process.

Focus on higher-order learning outcomes, such as application, analysis, synthesis, and evaluation, rather than on such lower-order outcomes as knowledge and comprehension. Make certain that evaluations favor students who achieve higher-order educational outcomes.

Model enthusiasm for the course content and for learning itself. Students assume that the instructor who habitually arrives late for class, seems preoccupied, reads directly from notes or from the book, and speaks in a monotone is bored with the class.

Give responsibility for learning back to the students. Allow them to design and select their learning experiences, topics, and methods of evaluation. Promote feelings of autonomy and personal involvement.

Avoid Extrinsic Motivators. Intrinsic motivation contrasts sharply with extrinsic motivation. Students, when intrinsically motivated, "experience interest and enjoyment, they feel competent and self-determining, they perceive the locus of causality for their behavior to be internal, and in some instances they experience flow" (Deci and Ryan, 1985, p. 34). When extrinsically motivated, by contrast, students are working for impersonal, external reasons. External motivators have a long history and possibly a permanent place in the classroom, but their negative impact on learning should be minimized, whenever possible, by basic precautions.

Use tests and other forms of evaluation to give students information about their accomplishments, but not to exert control or deny students' autonomy. Grades are the basic currency of the college classroom—the reward promised to students for good performance and the punishment threatened for failure. Instructors who stress tests, evaluations, and grades over all else, however, produce students who are striving to earn a particular grade rather than to learn the course material.

Exercise care when describing the need for grades, since even subtle nuances can influence motivation. Evaluations described as feedback to see how well students are doing have a less negative impact than evaluations designed to test whether they are performing as well as they should (Ryan, Mims, and Koestner, 1983). Similarly, students who are told that a grade of A means they are doing well in a subject perform better than students who are told that the A is a reward for working hard or for learning the material (Miller, Brickman, and Bolen, 1975).

Use the weakest extrinsic motivators possible. If you must use controlling methods—deadlines, pop quizzes, extra readings for poor performance, surveillance, penalties for nonattendance—then make certain that they are minimally sufficient to achieve compliance (Condry, 1987).

Minimize competition among students. Although introducing competition among students is a popular way to prompt them to expend greater effort, competition has many drawbacks. Competition focuses students' attention on winning, to the extent that they eventually conclude that "learning something new" is not nearly as important as "performing better than others" (Ames, 1987, p. 134). Failure in a competitive setting also undermines self-esteem and prompts students to blame their failures on lack of ability, rather than on lack of effort. Ames (1987), after thoroughly reviewing the literature, recommends excising all forms of competition from the college classroom by using criterion-based grading schemes (rather than norm-referenced schemes), by not posting grades and not grading on a curve, and by stressing the cooperative nature of learning.

Create a Mastery Orientation. Some of the most useful research into achievement motivation has been conducted by Dweck and her colleagues (Dweck, 1975; Dweck and Elliot, 1983; Dweck and Leggett, 1988). In her early research, Dweck found that students who think that their outcomes are within their control—mastery-oriented students—respond much differently from those who are helpless (Dweck and Licht, 1980; Dweck and Reppucci, 1973). After a failure, among mastery-oriented students, "effort is escalated, concentration is intensified, persistence is increased, strategy use becomes more sophisticated, and performance is enhanced"; by contrast, when helpless students fail, "efforts are curtailed, strategies deteriorate, and performance is often severely disrupted" (Dweck and Licht, 1980, p. 197). In one demonstration of these differences, Deiner and Dweck (1978) asked students who were failing on a cognitive task to "think out loud" about what they were doing. They discovered that 52 percent of the helpless questioned their ability, while none of the mastery-oriented students mentioned ability.

These findings suggest that instructors must remain sensitive to students' cognitive reactions to evaluations and test feedback. If students who do poorly in class conclude that there is nothing they personally can do to change their outcomes, then their failure may undermine their motivation and their satisfaction with themselves and academic work. If, however, the teacher encourages students to associate failure with factors that can be controlled, then the debilitating consequences of failure may be avoided. In addition, by emphasizing the importance of internal factors as causal agents after success, teachers may further ensure continued success. There are various methods for achieving this mastery orientation.

Encourage feelings of controllability in the classroom. Noel, Forsyth, and Kelley (1987) found that students who perform poorly often react very negatively and seek to blame their outcomes on lack of ability or on factors beyond their control: a poor teacher, a cold, a noisy roommate, and the like. Noel and his colleagues sought to undo these attributions by exposing some students to information that suggested that grades in college are caused by internal, controllable factors. The group was told, for example, that successful students generally believe they cause their own grades and have control over their performance. As predicted, on subsequent tests and on final examinations, these students earned higher grades than did control students who received no training.

Emphasize the extent to which grades and performance fluctuate over time. Wilson and Linville (1982, 1985), in studies of college students, succeeded in convincing first-year students that their grades were caused by unstable rather than stable factors. By comparison with "untreated" students, the students who were told that, on the average, college students do improve their grades during their educational careers were less likely to drop out at the end of the second year, and they achieved greater increases in their grade point averages.

Identify ways for students to increase their control over their outcomes. Do not just tell students they have control; give them control over their studying, the course material, and the way it is taught. For example, you can hold workshops on study skills, time management, and effective reading; provide students with important and useful resources, such as supplementary readings, an outline of your notes, and question-and-answer sessions; and allow students to take a role in designing evaluation procedures. If students realize that they can take behavioral steps to improve their performance, their sense of autonomy and control in the classroom should prosper.

Expectations for Success

In a tradition extending back to Tolman (1955), virtually all theories of human motivation argue that individuals intuitively calculate the probability that they will succeed in a particular situation. Although these calculations initially reflect generalized expectancies based on past performances, these generalized expectations are translated into more specific expectancies as the individual gains more and more information in the particular setting. Given that even students who are high in achievement orientation may not strive for success in classes where they expect to fail, teachers should maximize positive expectations, avoid fear of failure, and help shape their students' attributions about the causes of future performances.

Maximize Optimism Regarding Outcomes. The power of positive expectations is startling. As Rosenthal and Jacobson (1968) illustrate in their study of teachers' self-fulfilling prophecies, teachers who expect a student to succeed act in ways that make the student's success more likely. Moreover, students who develop positive expectations about their performance, by comparison with students who have bleaker expectations, work harder on class assignments, take a more active role in their learning by asking questions, learn more material, and come to think of themselves as high achievers (Harris and Rosenthal, 1985; Rosenthal, 1973). Merely expecting success in no way ensures success, but a positive expectation about performance is a crucial link in the motivation-achievement chain. This link can be made stronger if instructors take the following steps.

Develop positive expectations about students' chances of success. Rosenthal's (1973) work suggests that even instructors who try to keep their expectations private communicate these expectations to their students through subtle forms of behavior. Because negative expectations can become self-fulfilling prophecies, instructors should expect the most from their classes in general, and from specific individual students within the class. High expectations are communicated as instructors learn students' names and call on them by name, ask difficult, challenging questions, allow a long time for students to respond, provide helpful cues and prompts, and give warm, positive, non-verbal messages (Good and Brophy, 1986).

Avoid norm-referenced grading systems. When instructors grade on a curve, they ensure that some students in the class will earn failing grades. This grading scheme reinforces negative expectations, promotes competition among students, and limits the number of students who receive positive reinforcement.

Monitor the level of difficulty of tests and assignments. Evidence indicates that the perceived difficulty of the task is one of the primary determinants of subjective probability of success (Heckhausen, Schmalt, and Schneider, 1985). Students' expectations for success erode rapidly when instructors repeatedly give tests that are very difficult.

Provide students with encouraging information about future outcomes. Rather than tell students that most students fail a course at least once or that it will be the hardest course they will take in college, tell students how many people passed the course the last time you taught it or how many people improved their performance over time.

Minimize Fear of Failure. McClelland (1985) maintains that for some people, in some situations, the desire for success is replaced by the fear of failure. Individuals who fear failure tend to express negative attitudes toward achievement. They fail to set performance goals, they experience polarized emotional reactions when they succeed or fail, and they avoid evaluations if possible. As a result, they tend to become enmeshed in a negative cycle of low motivation that only serves to guarantee poor performance. This negative cycle can be short-circuited, however.

Limit the scope of the tasks attempted. Give many tests, rather than a few major tests, and provide opportunities to redress poor performance with good performance. Students should realize that a single poor performance will not do irreversible damage to their course grades.

Monitor the difficulty of the goals and tasks that students choose for themselves. Evidence indicates that individuals who are high in fear of failure tend to select tasks that are either so easy that they feel no pride in their accomplishments or so difficult that they are bound to fail (Heckhausen, Schmalt, and Schneider, 1985). Students should be counseled to select moderately difficult goals that they can reasonably expect to achieve. Moreover, if they fail to establish suitable goals, you can help them identify the paths that they can take to achieve such goals. When you include help sessions, study sheets, review sessions, and workshops on study skills in your teaching, students are more likely to feel that even moderately difficult goals can be achieved.

Minimize competition and social comparison in the classroom. In competitive settings, students often take steps to minimize their embarrassment over a failure, including deliberately refusing to study, cutting classes, or expressing derisive attitudes about the class content. These self-protective mechanisms, however, interfere substantially with performance and opportunities for success.

Actively attack negative expectations based on cultural stereotypes. Instructors must be particularly sensitive to the motivational needs of minorities and women. Instructors in college courses in areas that are traditionally viewed as male- or Anglo-dominated must undo these negative stereotypes; otherwise, students may not feel that they have the ability to meet course requirements (Bartz, 1984; Farmer, 1987; Maruyama, 1984).

Encourage Attributions to Controllable Causes. Motivation prospers when students feel that their outcomes are under their personal control. Feelings of control do not just increase general feelings of personal ability; they also increase students' expectations concerning success. When success is produced by factors that students think they can control—effort, motivation, diligence—they can assume that good scores will occur again. If, however, good grades are attributed to uncontrollable, external factors—such as an easy test, an excellent teacher, or the simplicity of the topic—then successful students must wonder whether they can maintain their high level of achievement. Conversely, failing students who believe that they can control the cause of their poor performance can reasonably hope to improve on future tasks. If, however, they believe that their grades result from uncontrollable factors, such as low ability or a poor teacher, their expectations concerning future outcomes will remain negative (Forsyth and McMillan, 1981). These attributional processes can be made to work in the service of motivation, however.

Minimize references to the causal importance of uncontrollable factors, such as mood, inspired guessing, time of year, luck, the ease or difficulty of the particular unit, the presence of poor items on the test, and so on. Instead, emphasize the causal impact on performance of effort, note-taking skill, diligence, preparation, and other factors. Irrespective of performance, students who think they control the causes of their outcomes experience more positive emotions than students who think their performance is caused by uncontrollable factors (Forsyth, 1986).

Provide differentiated feedback, rather than global feedback. Even when a student tests poorly, some questions that he or she answered correctly can be found. The student's ability to answer these items should be highlighted and explained by his or her superior learning of the material tested, rather than by the ease of the items.

Minimize the emotional repercussions of failure. Attributional reactions following failure are closely linked to emotional reactions (Weiner, 1985). Even when steps are taken to make certain that failure does not threaten self-esteem, students who perform poorly react very emotionally to their outcomes. The negative impacts of these emotional processes on motivation and on the quality of the classroom setting can be limited by discussing them in advance, avoiding confrontation in the classroom setting, and letting the feelings abate gradually over time.

Identifying Valuable Goals

Researchers exploring productivity in industrial settings discovered long ago the motivating power of goals. People working at jobs ranging from hauling logs to generating creative ideas to proofreading were found to be unproductive if their goals were vague or absent but productive if they were laboring to attain clearly established goals (Locke and Latham, 1990; Locke, Shaw, Saari, and Latham, 1981). These findings, applied to the classroom, suggest that students will perform better if they know what goals they are seeking and if those goals are personally important to them (Kleinbeck, Quast, and Schwarz, 1989).

Help Students Set Realistic Goals. Why do students take a particular class? Asking students this question can be a sobering experience for the college teacher. Such answers as "I want an A," "It meets at a good time," "It's required," "I have a friend in the class," or "I heard good things about the instructor" abound, whereas answers like "I'm seeking knowledge about this fascinating area" or "I think this material will be useful to me in my career" are relatively few.

Because goals are important sources of motivation, it may be worthwhile to spend time helping your students identify the goals they are seeking. This goal clarification can be achieved by discussing the goals of the class during the initial class session and including the goals of the class on the course syllabus. Using a brainstorming format, you can also develop a long list of goals through class discussion and then have students review the goals and suggest ways to achieve them. You can also arrange, as one of the class assignments, to have students identify their goals, or you can develop a simple goal-setting project that can be completed outside class. Whichever method you use to set goals, however, you should try to help students develop goals that are positive, behaviorally specific, realistic, and personally important (Danish, Galambos, and Laquatra, 1983).

Emphasize positive goals (things desired) rather than negative goals (things to avoid). Students should be encouraged to study more, rather than procrastinate less; take clearer notes, rather than not daydream during lectures; come to class, rather than skip class.

Goals that describe a specific behavioral outcome are superior to "do your best" goals or no goals. Particularly for students who are not doing well in the class, such goals as "Take two pages of well-organized notes" and "Read five pages and make a list of the key ideas in each section" are more effective motivators than "Get an A on the next test" or "Work hard."

Goals should be ones that the student, through effort, can attain. They should be challenging but not so difficult that the student will fail. Many educators recommend a mastery approach to goal setting, whereby students begin to work toward a goal only after they have attained the previous one.

Avoid giving students goals. Instead, ask each student to identify his or her own personal goals. When students generate their own goals, their intrinsic motivation is less likely to suffer, their commitment to the goals is greater, and, in most cases, the goals themselves are viewed as much more valuable (Locke, Shaw, Saari, and Latham, 1981).

As necessary, remind students of their goals. When goals are salient, learners process information more efficiently than when goals are unspecified; "from the wealth of information available to an individual in his environment, only those aspects of the environment that serve the goal-oriented control of action are registered and processed" (Kleinbeck, Quast, and Schwarz, 1989, p. 25). The learner, awash in a sea of information, must pick and choose what to remember and what to forget.

Help students develop strategies for achieving their goals. In many cases, students will need to develop coherent plans for attaining broad, overall goals. For example, they may need to break major goals into smaller sub-goals, or they may need to identify barriers that have prevented them from succeeding in the past.

Increase the Value of Academic Goals. Simply having a goal is not sufficient to produce increases in motivation. As expectancy-value theory argues, the motivational gains generated by goals depend to a large extent on the perceived value of the goals identified. A student, after identifying a series of positive, behaviorally specific, challenging goals, may still fail to work to achieve these goals if the goals are not viewed as personally meaningful or worthwhile.

Brophy (1987), drawing on analyses of classroom motivation, offers a number of recommendations aimed at increasing the attractiveness of educational outcomes. These recommendations, some of which are incorporated into the following paragraphs, work by changing students' perceptions of the course material and providing them with overarching goals related to the class and the educational experience.

Model enthusiasm and interest in the topic and in learning. Social learning theory recommends increasing the value of educational outcomes by providing an example for students (Bandura, 1977). Instructors who are interested in the material, who display a scholarly attitude while teaching, and who seem genuinely interested in achieving understanding are more likely to produce students who also display these values.

Expect interest, not boredom. Brophy notes that students will rise to the level of their instructors' expectations. If teachers think the students will find the material boring, then students typically react with indifference and boredom. If, however, teachers treat students as "active, motivated learners who care about their learning and are trying to understand" (Brophy, 1987, p. 195), then positive motivation is much more likely (Good and Brophy, 1986).

Directly address the importance of each new topic examined. When beginning a new subject, assigning a task, or asking students to read a chapter, highlight the value of the learning activity with a short overview. For example, explain the scholar's excitement over the particular topic ("When Darwin published *The Origin of Species,* the scientific community reeled"), your own interest in the material and how it relates to some personal incident in your life ("I first read *The Old Man and the Sea* when my family was vacationing at the shore"), the practical utility of the information about to be presented ("The principle of supply and demand explains why all the things you buy each day—from a cola to a fast-food burger—cost what they do"), or the long-term usefulness of a working knowledge of the topic ("Many of the ideas we have discussed so far will be of use to you in your career, but the principles of forecasting are perhaps the most essential"). Be careful, however, in phrasing your message (Brophy and Kher, 1986). Brophy found that even when teachers take the time to tell students that the upcoming material is stimulating and personally useful in the long run, they accidentally include threatening information as well. The teacher who says, "Once we finish this section, we will understand some of the puzzles that challenged even Plato and Socrates" is also likely to say, "It is so important that we will have a quiz next session to test your comprehension."

Make the material personally relevant to students. Novel, challenging, or unfamiliar ideas are more interesting to learners when they are tied to more familiar, personally relevant ideas. According to Brophy (1987, p. 197), "Teachers can promote personal identification with the content by relating experiences or telling anecdotes illustrating how the content applies to the lives of particular individuals."

Select topics and tasks that interest students. If you have the choice to teach one of two equally worthwhile topics, select the topic that students will find more enjoyable and exciting. When a number of methods can be used to accomplish a particular learning outcome, show a preference for methods that match students' existing interests. Allow students to choose among various options. Use novel introductions and activities that diverge from your usual method of teaching, and allow students to learn actively rather than passively. When you can, tie class activities and content to significant features of students' lives. Students' concerns about interpersonal relationships, for example, can be used to stimulate discussion about fundamental biological processes, research methods in psychology, changing views of love in art, sociological conceptions of the basis of political structures, and so on.

Take time to understand what students perceive as important and interesting. All too often, professors assume that they know what will be challenging or stimulating. Stress the importance of students' involvement in meaningful learning, and ask them to evaluate activities and content on this basis. If students do not agree with you, ask them to generate further options.

Summary

Motivation is, to a large extent, a basic dispositional quality of each learner, but savvy instructors can do much to raise motivation by structuring their classrooms carefully. The practical suggestions we have presented are based on theory, research, and our experiences as teachers. If we can keep students intrinsically motivated, provide meaningful feedback, and encourage the development of realistic, valuable, and achievable goals that students expect to achieve, their engagement in learning should be enhanced.

References

Ames, C. "The Enhancement of Student Motivation." In M. L. Maehr and D. A. Kleiber (eds.), *Advances in Motivation and Achievement.* Vol. 5. *Enhancing Motivation.* Greenwich, Conn.: JAI Press, 1987.

Bandura, A. *Social Learning Theory.* Englewood Cliffs, N.J.: Prentice-Hall, 1977.

Bartz, D. E. "Remediating Social and Psychological Harm Resulting from Segregative Acts." In D. E. Bartz and M. L. Maehr (eds.), *Advances in Motivation and Achievement.* Vol. 1. Greenwich, Conn.: JAI Press, 1984.

Brophy, J. "Socializing Students' Motivation to Learn." In M. L. Maehr and D. Kleiber (eds.), *Advances in Motivation and Achievement.* Vol. 5. *Enhancing Motivation.* Greenwich, Conn.: JAI Press, 1987.

Brophy, J., and Kher, N. "Teacher Socialization as a Mechanism for Developing Student Motivation to Learn." In R. Feldman (ed.), *Social Psychology Applied to Education.* New York: Cambridge University Press, 1986.

Carver, C. S., and Scheier, M. F. *Attention and Self-Regulation: A Control-Theory Approach to Human Behavior.* New York: Springer-Verlag, 1981.

Condry, J. "Enhancing Motivation: A Social Developmental Perspective." In M. L. Maehr and D. A. Kleiber (eds.), *Advances in Motivation and Achievement.* Vol. 5. *Enhancing Motivation.* Greenwich, Conn.: JAI Press, 1987.

Danish, S. J., Galambos, N. L., and Laquatra, I. "Life Development Interventions: Skill Training for Personal Competence." In R. D. Felner, L. A. Jason, J. N. Maritsugu, and S. S. Farber (eds.), *Preventive Psychology: Theory, Research, and Practice.* New York: Pergamon Press, 1983.

deCharms, R. *Enhancing Motivation.* New York: Irvington, 1976.

deCharms, R. "The Burden of Motivation." In M. L. Maehr and D. A. Kleiber (eds.), *Advances in Motivation and Achievement.* Vol. 5. *Enhancing Motivation.* Greenwich, Conn.: JAI Press, 1987.

Deci, E. L., and Ryan, R. M. *Intrinsic Motivation and Self-Determination in Human Behavior.* New York: Plenum, 1985.

Diener, C. I., and Dweck, C. S. "An Analysis of Learned Helplessness: Continuous Changes in Performance, Strategy, and Achievement Cognitions Following Failure." *Journal of Personality and Social Psychology,* 1978, *36,* 451–462.

Dweck, C. S. "The Role of Expectations and Attributions in the Alleviation of Learned Helplessness." *Journal of Personality and Social Psychology,* 1975, *31,* 674–685.

Dweck, C. S., and Elliot, E. S. "Achievement Motivation." In E. M. Hetherington (ed.), *Handbook of Child Psychology.* Vol. 4. *Social and Personality Development.* (4th ed.) New York: Wiley, 1983.

Dweck, C., and Leggett, E. L. "A Social-Cognitive Approach to Motivation and Personality." *Psychological Bulletin,* 1988, *95,* 256–273.

Dweck, C. S., and Licht, B. G. "Learned Helplessness and Intellectual Achievement." In M.E.P. Seligman and J. Garber (eds.), *Human Helplessness: Theory and Application.* Orlando, Fla.: Academic Press, 1980.

Dweck, C. S., and Reppucci, N. D. "Learned Helplessness and Reinforcement of Responsibility in Children." *Journal of Personality and Social Psychology,* 1973, *25,* 109–116.

Farmer, H. S. "Female Motivation and Achievement: Implications for Interventions." In M. L. Maehr and D. A. Kleiber (eds.), *Advances in Motivation and Achievement.* Vol. 5. *Enhancing Motivation.* Greenwich, Conn.: JAI Press, 1987.

Forsyth, D. R. "An Attributional Analysis of Students' Reactions to Success and Failure." In R. S. Feldman (ed.), *The Social Psychology of Education.* New York: Cambridge University Press, 1986.

Forsyth, D. R., and McMillan, J. H. "Attributions, Affect, and Expectations: A Test of Weiner's Three-Dimensional Model." *Journal of Educational Psychology,* 1981, *73,* 393–401.

Good, T. L., and Brophy, J. E. *Educational Psychology: A Realistic Approach.* (3rd ed.) New York: Longman, 1986.

Harris, M. J., and Rosenthal, R. "Mediation of Interpersonal Expectancy Effects." *Psychological Bulletin,* 1985, *97,* 363–386.

Heckhausen, H., Schmalt, H-D., and Schneider, K. *Achievement Motivation in Perspective.* Orlando, Fla.: Academic Press, 1985.

Kleinbeck, U., Quast, H., and Schwarz, R. "Volitional Effects on Performance: Conceptual Considerations and Results from Dual-Task Studies." In R. Kanfer, P. L. Ackerman, and R. Cudeck (eds.), *Abilities, Motivation, and Methodology: The Minnesota Symposium on Learning and Individual Differences.* Hillsdale, N.J.: Erlbaum, 1989.

Lepper, M. "Extrinsic Reward and Intrinsic Motivation: Implications for the Classroom." In J. Levine and M. Wang (eds.), *Teacher and Student Perspectives: Implications for Learning.* Hillsdale, N.J.: Erlbaum, 1983.

Locke, E. A., and Latham, G. P. "Work Motivation and Satisfaction: Light at the End of the Tunnel." *Psychological Science,* 1990, *1,* 240–246.

Locke, E. A., Shaw, K. N., Saari, L. M., and Latham, G. P. "Goal Setting and Task Performance: 1969–1980." *Psychological Bulletin,* 1981, *90,* 125–152.

McClelland, D. C. *Human Motivation.* Glenview, Ill.: Scott, Foresman, 1985.

Maruyama, G. "What Causes Achievement? An Examination of Antecedents in Segregated and Desegregated Classrooms." In D. E. Bartz and M. L. Maehr (eds.), *Advances in Motivation and Achievement.* Vol. 1. Greenwich, Conn.: JAI Press, 1984.

Miller, R. L., Brickman, P., and Bolen, D. "Attribution Versus Persuasion as a Means for Modifying Behavior." *Journal of Personality and Social Psychology*, 1975, *31*, 430–441.

Noel, J., Forsyth, D. R., and Kelley, K. N. "Improving the Performance of Failing Students by Overcoming Their Self-Serving Attributional Biases." *Basic and Applied Social Psychology*, 1987, *8*, 151–162.

Purkey, W. W. *Self-Concept and School Achievement.* Englewood Cliffs, N.J.: Prentice-Hall, 1970.

Rosenthal, R. "The Mediation of Pygmalion Effects: A Four-Factor 'Theory.' " *Papua New Guinea Journal of Education*, 1973, *9*, 1–12.

Rosenthal, R., and Jacobson, L. *Pygmalion in the Classroom: Teacher Expectation and Pupils' Intellectual Development.* New York: Holt, Rinehart & Winston, 1968.

Rotter, J. B. "Generalized Expectancies for Internal Versus External Control of Reinforcement." *Psychological Monographs*, 1966, *80* (entire issue 1).

Ryan, R. M., Mims, V., and Koestner, R. "Relation of Reward Contingency and Interpersonal Context to Intrinsic Motivation: A Review and Test Using Cognitive Evaluation Theory." *Journal of Personality and Social Psychology*, 1983, *45*, 736–750.

Tolman, E. C. "Principles of Performance." *Psychological Review*, 1955, *62*, 315–326.

Weiner, B. "An Attributional Theory of Achievement Motivation and Emotion." *Psychological Review*, 1985, *92*, 548–573.

White, R. M. "Motivation Reconsidered: The Concept of Competence." *Psychological Review*, 1959, *66*, 297–333.

Wilson, T. D., and Linville, P. W. "Improving the Academic Performance of College Freshmen: Attribution Therapy Revisited." *Journal of Personality and Social Psychology*, 1982, *42*, 367–376.

Wilson, T. D., and Linville, P. W. "Improving the Academic Performance of College Freshmen with Attributional Techniques." *Journal of Personality and Social Psychology*, 1985, *49*, 287–293.

Donelson R. Forsyth is director of undergraduate studies and professor in the Department of Psychology, Virginia Commonwealth University. He is currently researching the attributional and emotional consequences of students' reactions to their academic successes and failures.

James H. McMillan is associate professor of educational studies at Virginia Commonwealth University. His interests include motivation and learning of college students and assessment of educational outcomes.

The social context of teaching and learning is gaining recognition as an important component of teaching effectiveness. The social context is also a central feature of several major contemporary approaches to education.

The Social Context of Teaching and Learning

Richard G. Tiberius, Janet Mancini Billson

> Technology has built the house in which we all live. . . . I myself am overawed by the way in which technology has acted to reorder and restructure social relations. . . .
> —Ursula Franklin (1990, pp. 11, 13)

People have been learning and teaching since the origin of our species. Stone Age children survived by watching their elders pick berries or smash bones, and those who guided their little hands were among the first teachers. However, for these early teachers, teaching was not the distinct activity that it is today. It was simply a part of normal life, of routine social interaction.

Even today, very young children absorb an impressive array of values, norms, behavioral patterns, and information through informal interaction with their caregivers, and countless adult-learning projects are embedded in the normal social context that comprises everyday living. Tough (1977) has reviewed studies showing that between 70 and 100 percent of American adults are involved in at least one major learning effort every year, and 80 percent of such projects are not planned by formal learning institutions.

By contrast, formal education appears to be alienated from its social context. What happened? We are compelled by Franklin's (1990) explanation that normal social relations, including the social context of teaching and learning, have been profoundly influenced by the dominant force of our age: high technology. With the proliferation of the specialized roles that were essential to the division of labor during the Industrial Revolution, teaching, like many other occupations, became highly circumscribed work, conducted by trained and certified professionals in particular locations (schools of various sorts). The natural interaction that sustained motivation and personal relationships, and which was the vehicle for essential feedback between teachers and students, has been replaced by prescribed behaviors and roles for teachers and students. The teacher as expert has led to teacher-student relationships marked by formalism, distance, and authority.

By *social context,* we mean the entire spectrum of roles, responsibilities, expectations, and interactions between students and teachers, and among students. The social context is inherent in every teaching situation, from the standard lecture or organized tutorial session to the study group or interactive, cooperative class. It is not totally under the control of either faculty or students but results from interaction and is influenced by the institutional setting and the larger social context as well.

Contemporary theorists, such as Schön (1987) and Cross (1988), assert that effective teacher-student interaction does not result from the enactment of skilled performances by the teacher alone, but rather from a restructuring of the social arrangements between teachers and students and among students. We concur. However, progress in moving toward effective social arrangements for teaching and learning, we believe, has been impaired by the dominant metaphors of education, which are prescriptive and product-oriented. A recent review of the educational development literature (Tiberius, 1986) identifies two metaphors of the teaching-and-learning process—the metaphor of teaching as transmission of information, and the metaphor of dialogue (or conversation). The dialogue metaphor emphasizes "the interactive, cooperative, and relational aspects of teaching and learning" (Tiberius, 1986, p. 148). The teacher becomes a facilitator of students' learning and a learner in the process.

Fox (1983) identifies a similar polarity in metaphors held by university teachers. He found that some teachers view their role as transmitting information or shaping students, while others view it as helping students grow. Franklin (1990) also distinguishes between a "production" metaphor and a "growth" metaphor, concepts parallel to those of transmission and dialogue. She argues that a growth metaphor is a more appropriate guide to learning and teaching than a production metaphor is. Learning is not a product that can be controlled; it can only be encouraged or facilitated. A production model strives to make measurable, quantifiable outcomes achievable in a climate of control, planning, and pressure of resources and time; but "growth occurs; it is not made" (Franklin, 1990, p. 27). Unfortunately, the metaphor of teaching as transmission of information still dominates over metaphors of dialogue or conversation.

What are the features of a social context for teaching and learning that could assist us in making the shift from the production metaphor to the dialogue metaphor? In this chapter, we review some of the theoretical and empirical approaches bearing on this question and attempt to identify some of their common features. In the next chapter, we suggest practical methods for creating, maintaining, and restoring effective social arrangements for teaching and learning in higher education.

Several key features of a social context that fosters student learning and growth emerge from our review of the literature: mutual respect, a shared responsibility for learning and mutual commitment to goals, effective communication and feedback, cooperation and a willingness to negotiate conflicts, and a sense of security in the classroom. These features appear to form a coherent ideal for the social arrangements between teachers and students, an ideal we refer to as the *alliance* (see Tiberius and others, 1989). These defining features determine the strength of the alliance, and they influence the achievement of such outcomes as attitudes and learning. (Some writers use the word *relationship* to signify what we mean by the *alliance;* we believe that *relationship* is too narrow and that *alliance* carries a more positive, intentional implication.)

Importance of the Social Context of Teaching and Learning

The social context has importance beyond the learning and growth that take place in the immediate teacher-student alliance. The social arrangements between teachers and students have implications for both student development and teacher development. Several researchers have found that the teacher-student relationship can have positive effects on student development, including academic achievement, intellectual development, persistence in higher education, personality development, and educational aspirations (Pascarella, 1980; Terenzini and Pascarella, 1980; Volkwein, King, and Terenzini, 1986). Although not all teacher-student contact is associated with such positive outcomes, students who are positively connected with their teachers are more likely to feel involved in their educational experience, to be committed to the institution, to have passing grades, and to persist to graduation (Billson, 1982). Opportunities for meaningful advisement, development of friendships, and testing of ideas and talents are affected by the social context. Teacher-student interaction is more influential if it is characterized by concern for student development and for teaching.

Rogers (1969), an early proponent of the significance of the social context, argued that learning does not depend simply on the teacher's leadership skills, scholarly knowledge, planning skills, use of audiovisual aids, programmed learning, lecturing ability, or books; "the facilitation of significant learning rests upon certain attitudinal qualities which exist in the personal relationship between the facilitator and the learner" (Rogers, 1969, pp. 105–106). Since this insight, there has been increasing recognition of the importance of the social context. Recent reviews of the literature that aim to identify the principles underlying teaching and learning have substantiated the major importance of the social context. In a study co-sponsored by the American Association for Higher Education and the Education Commission of the States (Chickering and Gamson, 1989), seven principles of good practice in undergraduate education were extracted from fifty years of research on teaching and learning: the effective teacher encourages contacts between students and faculty, develops reciprocity and cooperation among students, uses active learning techniques, gives prompt feedback, emphasizes time on task, communicates high expectations, and respects diverse talents and ways of learning. Many of these general principles are related to the social context of teaching and learning.

Lowman's (1984) search for the key characteristics of successful teaching led to the conclusion that they fall naturally into two fundamental categories: clarity of presentation, and quality of interpersonal relations. The literature on teaching and learning gives them about equal weight in their influence on teaching effectiveness.

Approaches and Perspectives

A number of research and conceptual approaches to teaching and learning address the social context, at least indirectly. We comment briefly on six: the transactional perspective, student-centered instruction, cooperative learning, communication theory, group-process theory, and curricular/structural approaches.

The Transactional Perspective. An early contribution to this perspective was designed by Rosenblatt (1956) specifically for teaching English literature in college. Her method, which emphasized students' own responses to the text, rather than their answers to teachers' questions, was based on two principles: that students are naturally motivated to understand their own responses to a text, and that meaning is made, not found (Probst, 1981).

Darnell (1978) made the first systematic attempt to apply the transactional perspective to the arena of teaching and learning. This perspective, which grew out of communication theory, "emphasizes the interdependence of the participating elements in the process and the inherent unpredictability of the outcome of the process, and de-emphasizes the intentional control of the process by one of the participating parties" (Darnell, 1978, p. 277). Darnell challenged the model of teaching in which the teacher controls students by manipulating rewards. He questioned the assumption that students learn only what they are taught and learn from external experience (lectures, reading). A teacher who held such assumptions would emphasize control of the environment and would blame the instructional method if the educational program failed to work. According to the transactional perspective, these assumptions are false. Rewards can be counterproductive; students are learning all the time, whether or not they are being taught in any formal sense; and students learn from internal experience (they learn from their private interpretation of external experience). A teacher who operated from the transactional perspective would probably enter into cooperative interaction with students. The teacher would be concerned with how students interpreted the educational experience, through developing relationships of trust in which students can openly express frustrations and accomplishments, hopes and expectations.

External control, in the form of bribes, rewards, and threats, may have some immediate desirable effects on performance, but it may also have unfortunate consequences, as far as motivation is concerned. Darnell (1978) cites a number of studies to refute the idea that the more inducements we offer students, the more students do what we want them to do, continue doing it, and learn what we want them to learn. He argues that we should "opt for minimum external control so that students will have a chance to develop internal control" (p. 283) necessary for real-world rather than classroom performance. Darnell also recognizes that with students whose motivation is very low, it may be necessary to enhance short-term motivation, regardless of the long-term effects. In such cases, he advises motivating students by getting to know them individually and appealing to their unique interests and needs. The moral superiority, as well as the effectiveness, of this individual approach to motivation has been supported (see Tiberius, 1974).

It appears that the application of the transactional process to higher education has not been pursued in the literature. However, the main ideas of this approach are reappearing in a relatively new approach to teaching called *reciprocal teaching*. According to Palincsar, Ransom, and Derber (1989), students and teachers who engage in reciprocal teaching enter into dialogue about the meaning of a text, taking turns in a shared responsibility for the conversation's quality and direction. They generate questions about the text, summarize, clarify points, and predict upcoming content. At first, the teacher takes the major responsibility for demonstrating the strategies, but gradually the teacher releases control of the dialogue to the students. Compared to traditional methods, the method is effective and efficient.

Miller, Miller, and Rosen (1988) attribute the superior performance of reciprocal teaching to several factors, including active involvement of students when they take the role of teacher. Students engaged in reciprocal learning summarize, identify key words, ask questions, and require more paraphrasing than students in the traditional learning condition. Such active learning processes may enable students to encode the ideas in ways that have more meaning to them, and to clarify misunderstandings through discussion.

Although Palincsar, Ransom, and Derber (1989) were apparently unaware of it, Darnell had already described a reciprocal teaching method similar to their own. Darnell (1978) describes a student's paper or project as he sees it and then asks the student to describe the same project to him. They frequently discover that they are talking about (evaluating) two quite different things. If each respects the other's viewpoint, the incongruity is dissipated, and they can negotiate a mutually acceptable evaluation. The process can be time-consuming and uncomfortable for student and teacher alike, but they both "often learn more from this than from producing and grading the paper or project in the first place" (Darnell, 1978, p. 284).

A relatively large body of experimental literature documents the effectiveness of reciprocal interaction as a study technique between pairs of students. This work has been associated primarily with Dansereau (see Larson and Dansereau, 1986): after reversing roles several times during a reciprocal teaching exercise, students learned how to become teachers and were able to teach one another in the manner described by Dansereau. The teacher teaches by example, in stark contrast to the "control" strategy, which has teachers didactically telling students how to cooperate among themselves. Although this research is concerned with interaction between students rather than between teachers and students, there is evidence that these learning techniques can be developed as a natural outgrowth of interactive relationships between teachers and learners. Such a development is precisely what Palincsar, Ransom, and Derber (1989) described in the reciprocal teaching program.

Learner-Centered, Self-Directed Instruction. The power of the social context is implied by recent research on learner-centered instruction. Relatively minor accommodation to students—consisting of teachers' smiling and joking—has a significant positive influence on the interpersonal climate, even when students are sitting and listening to lectures.

Rogers (1983) has reviewed empirical literature to support the conclusion that such student behaviors as talking, involvement, and initiation and such teacher behaviors as smiling, sensitivity to feelings, and use of students' ideas all promote effective learning and personal growth. Murray (1983) and Erdle, Murray, and Rushton (1985) have found that smiling and a sense of humor, expressed in lectures, are correlated with high student ratings. Cranton and Hillgartner (1981) found such characteristics as teachers' enthusiasm and rapport to be responsible for greater learning and a more positive attitude toward teachers.

Greeson (1985, 1986, 1988) goes much farther toward accommodation of the learner. According to Greeson, effective social arrangements are not merely things that teachers do but are different ways that teachers and students relate to one another. Greeson's studies are concerned with the broader social arrangements between teacher and student. His examination of teachers' and students' behavior under both student-centered and teacher-centered instruction indicates that student-centered instruction can enhance "the dynamics of interaction between teachers and learners in classroom settings" (Greeson, 1988, p. 314).

Greeson (1988) compared two courses taught by the same teacher. One was an introductory psychology course, taught in the traditional teacher-centered manner, with lectures, standard assignments, quizzes, tests, and grades. The other was a student-centered, self-directed section, taught with periodic personal goal setting, monitoring conferences, informal group-discussion tests, and grades determined by mutual agreement. The final grades of the students taught by the two approaches were not statistically different, but the student-centered method was rated consistently higher by the students than the teacher-centered approach was. Greeson's design for student-centered instruction represented a radically different pattern of interaction, compared to the teacher-centered instruction. In the student-centered section, teachers talked significantly less than teachers in the teacher-centered section; students initiated more questions, shared information more frequently among themselves, and generated more ideas. The student-centered condition was characterized by reciprocity, negotiation, and a sharing of the responsibility for learning (Greeson, 1988).

Learner-centered instruction is aimed at increasing the responsibility of the learner. In our view, learner-centered instruction should not overwhelm other educational strategies. Instruction that is completely learner-centered would mean learners struggling on their own, without the help of a teacher. Learner-centered approaches are popular today as a welcome corrective to other methods; their popularity attests to how skewed instruction in higher education has become toward teacher-centeredness. (For reviews of other studies of learner-centered instruction, see McKeachie, Pintrich, Lin, and Smith, 1986.)

Cooperative Teaching and Learning. The cooperative learning perspective, which is currently moving from K–12 into higher education, promises to change dramatically the social arrangements between teachers and students. Cooperative learning is an instructional strategy in which small groups work toward a common goal (Cooper and Mueck, 1989). The main features of cooperative learning have been summarized by Millis (1990): positive interdependence (all members of the group contribute to one another's learning); individual accountability (no student can ride free on the labor of others, because course grades largely reflect individual learning); heterogeneous teams (a mixture of students represents differences in learning abilities, ethnic diversity, and gender); group processing (such activities as reflecting on the group's effectiveness are designed to build team skills); and social skills (to help students engage in cooperative interaction and show mutual respect). Although most of the research documenting the advantages of cooperative learning has been conducted so far in K–12 settings (Slavin, 1989–90), recent college-based research supports similar conclusions: cooperative learning is more effective, more fun, and leads to greater student involvement and cooperative group skills (Millis, 1990).

The teacher's role in cooperative learning is expanded beyond the typical "product" model of simply presenting information and evaluating. Teachers, as necessary, may present minilectures, but their main function is to facilitate—to set tasks for the group and guide the group toward cooperation, trust, and interdependence. The responsibility for learning is shifted from the teacher's shoulders (see Finkel and Monk, 1983) to the students'; the teacher becomes coach rather than expert (see Schön, 1987). The teacher's role in cooperative learning has been linked with Rogers's person-centered theory (Hassard, 1990, p. ix): "It requires a conscious shift of perspective on the part of the teacher, away from authoritarianism and toward coordination of cooperative actions and the facilitation of instruction. Teachers who have incorporated this philosophy into their classrooms orchestrate the students' activities and are masters in securing and creating well-designed, team-oriented tasks."

Communication Theory. Perhaps the most relevant treatment of communication for our purposes is the social interaction theory of Watzlawick, Beavin, and Jackson (1967). They argue that "every communication has a content and a relationship aspect such that the latter classifies the former" (p. 54). Since messages are contained within contexts consisting of human relationships, the meaning of a message is inherently dependent on this context. This theory has been applied to the classroom by Simpson and Galbo (1986), who discuss the influence of relationships on communication.

If the quality of the relationship is as important to communication as Simpson and Galbo (1986) argue, then the formation of an alliance between teacher and students is important to efficient communication. Moreover, it appears that communication aimed at forming a stable relationship directly contributes to effectiveness. Perhaps this explains why informal interaction between teacher and students is associated with positive outcomes (Pascarella, 1980).

Simpson and Galbo (1986) apply to teaching and learning another idea from the Watzlawick theory that points to the importance of the alliance: the result of any communication is a function of the unique interaction at the time it takes place. The meaning is created out of the dynamics of the situation, not only from the content but also from what each actor brings to the situation: "The quality of a particular interaction is not entirely predictable, for the ultimate form is determined by the participants at the time of the encounter. Thus, teachers cannot determine with certainty how students will respond to the various parts of a lesson plan. They must rely upon information gained through interacting with students during the lesson to determine some of the ultimate specifics of instruction" (Simpson and Galbo, 1986, pp. 49–50).

Seeking and using information on the spot during teaching is a high-level professional skill that is little understood and poorly researched, according to Simpson and Galbo (1986). They view the personality of the teacher as the instrument of instruction, in ways that the teacher may not fully recognize; effective teachers know how to use their personalities to stimulate connections between students' prior experiences and the subject matter. In traditional approaches to teaching effectiveness, the personality variable is considered "noise" in the system. Researchers seek methods that are independent of personality. Simpson and Galbo (1986, p. 51) turn the traditional assumption on its head: "Much of the research about classroom instruction has attempted to control the teacher's personality as a variable. . . . the more productive course of action may be to control for method and to make the teacher's personality the experimental variable."

Jones (1989) found that student ratings of teachers' competence depend on their perceptions of teachers' personalities as well as of their technical competence: the importance of personality is valid, not a contamination of ratings data. He says that "students across a wide range of ages and institutions typically report two types of factors which they associate with good teachers: technical and personological factors. [By personological aspects, he means those that humanize the classroom and help students achieve a feeling of self-worth.] If you like someone, you start relating to [him], can identify with [him], and are in a position of being prepared to learn from [him]" (Jones, 1989, p. 557).

DeVito (1986) takes the next logical step, placing the development of the teacher-student relationship at the center of the educational process. The primary assumption of DeVito's "relational" approach to teaching is that teaching can best be understood and improved by our defining it as a process of relational development. He presents nine relationship skills—emphasizing openness, empathy, supportiveness, equality, cooperation, trust, and interaction—that can help teachers enhance their effectiveness. Teachers should encourage meaningful dialogue and serve as models for students in encouraging dialogue; seek feedback from others to find out how accurately they are being perceived; be able to relinquish control to students; listen actively; decipher relational as well as content messages; develop sensitivity to the verbal and nonverbal aspects of messages; and be able to repair relationships.

Another central theme of communication theory centers on feedback. Feedback is considered one of the central mechanisms of experiential learning and action research (Kolb, 1984), sensitivity training (Lakin, 1972), and laboratory methods of personal and organizational change (Schein and Bennis, 1965). Research shows that both teaching and learning are enhanced by descriptive feedback that occurs in the course of interaction between teachers and students. This is true in the dyadic teacher-student relationship (as in tutoring or advising) and in the classroom group. Billson (1986) cites research showing that group interaction is integrally linked to feedback. On the cognitive level, Guskey (1988) points to the critical role that feedback plays in mastery learning. When students are given the scope to define issues, problems, and projects, work can be broken into discrete blocks that can be targeted, attempted, and mastered, with many opportunities for immediate feedback, criticism, redirection, and consultation.

Contrast these personal approaches to teaching with approaches, such as televised lectures, that have no possibility for interaction or mutual accommodation. Scarborough College, the first North American college designed for television, was expected to realize a 30 percent reduction in professor hours and savings of millions of dollars (Lee, 1971). After a few years, the program collapsed. An important factor in its demise was the unhappiness of students with "talking heads." They wanted teachers who could respond to them. Televised teachers could not respond in subsequent lectures to students' reactions. This lack of reciprocal communication was just as deadening in a video performance as it would have been in an insensitive live lecturer.

Wing (1990), after a review of the research on feedback, concludes that feedback will not promote learning unless at least two conditions are met: the recipient must have a performance goal, and the goal must be the same as that of the provider of the feedback. These conditions have implications for any feedback that is intended to improve the social context, and they apply both to students' evaluations of teachers and to teachers' evaluation of students.

Common forms of feedback to students include end-of-semester exams and papers. Since it is too late then for students to alter their performance (hence, their grades), the recipient of the evaluation does not have a performance goal. (This is also true for any evaluation of written work during the semester that does not allow for at least one draft.) Similarly, the most common form of feedback to improve teaching—student ratings at the end of the term—also usually violates Wing's (1990) principles. The popularity of this method is fueled by the assumption that, in order to improve, teachers need only one thing: accurate information about the success or failure of their teaching strategies. Such information, it is believed, should enable teachers to correct their teaching errors. In our experience, ratings often come too late to build or change the alliance, or they provide information that is not relevant to a teacher's personal teaching goals.

Each teacher must learn to develop a style and use his or her personality effectively, in a unique way. Individual improvement of this sort cannot be achieved through correction toward a standardized teaching performance. This uniqueness helps to explain the finding that when ratings feedback is coupled with individual consulting, it is four times as effective (Menges and Brinko, 1986).

There is also evidence that the impact of ratings on teaching effectiveness can be enhanced significantly (without the advice of a consultant) by adding feedback in the form of discussions with students (Tiberius and others, 1989). In this study, feedback consisted of discussions, with small groups of students, conducted by a skilled group leader and directed toward comprehensive, candid evaluation of a teacher's performance. The authors explain their results in terms of the social context of teaching and learning: "Teaching and learning is a collaborative venture which depends for its success on an agreement (sometimes explicit, but most often implicit) between teachers and students to work together toward common educational objectives. Certain attitudes and responses appear to be essential to the success of this collaborative interaction. Students respond much more enthusiastically to teachers whom they regard as genuinely interested in them and committed to teaching them. And teachers respond much more enthusiastically to students whom they perceive as eager to learn" (Tiberius and others, 1989, p. 679). This study indicates that relational issues are not peripheral to the teaching process but central to it.

Group-Process Theory. At the heart of the alliance, mutual commitment implies that both teachers and students take responsibility for the outcome of their joint interaction. This implies reciprocity, bilateral leadership, and shared investment in what takes place in the educational relationship.

A central principle of effective group interaction is that every participant is responsible for its outcome. This principle applies to the dyadic group formed by the teacher and the student in tutorial or advisement settings, and to teacher-student interaction in the classroom group. Since students are members of the classroom group, their responsibility for class interaction is reciprocally intertwined with the teacher's (Billson, 1986).

Group morale, cohesion, solidarity, and effective problem solving depend on the achievement of a balance between instrumental (task) and socioemotional (affective) functions (Slater, 1955; Bales and Slater, 1955). A group leader who attends to such task issues as goal setting, timing, productivity, and division of labor, without also attending to how group members feel about participating in the group, risks inhibiting the overall group success. The most effective leaders, Slater and Bales have both argued, pay as much attention to resolving conflicts, ensuring even participation, and testing group sentiment as they do to planning, keeping the group on task, and evaluating productivity. Similarly, Forsyth (1990) claims that all small groups have two basic objectives: task completion and maintenance of collaborative relationships among members.

Achieving balance between these two areas is a central problem of group life. Both areas are essential to successful accomplishment of the work of the group. An analysis of balanced leadership suggests that the following roles must be carried out effectively (adapted from Miles, 1973, p. 20, and from Beebe and Masterson, 1986, pp. 216–220):

Initiating: getting group action off the ground (suggesting actions, pointing out a goal, proposing a procedure)

Regulating: influencing the direction and tempo of the group's work (restating goals, pointing out time limits)

Informing: bringing information or opinion to the group

Evaluating: helping the group evaluate its progress, goals, or procedures (testing for consensus, noting group progress)

Coordinating: helping the group explore relationships among individual contributions (assisting with team building and division of labor on group projects)

Summarizing: helping the group stay on track, in terms of task and content (showing how far discussion has progressed, indicating possible directions for proceeding)

Elaborating: helping the group clarify, expand, and refine ideas for further discussion

Supporting: creating an emotional climate that makes it easy for members to contribute to the task (relieving tension, voicing group feeling, encouraging)

Gatekeeping: ensuring that participation is kept open to all members of the class, avoiding monopolization of discussion by dominants

Mediating: facilitating conflict resolution, negotiating compromises, shifting discussion away from personalities and emotions and toward ideas and conceptualization.

Even though task and socioemotional functions can be separated conceptually, in fact they are intertwined. A teacher who performs well in the first five roles—task areas—will also be contributing greatly to morale, positive climate, and satisfaction. Conversely, if a teacher is too concerned with initiating or informing, to the neglect of other roles, the class will have difficulty in achieving its task goals because morale will be lowered. A teacher who fails to negotiate clear expectations, is disorganized, or does not move the class toward achieving its stated goals is performing inadequately in the task role. The teacher in a small-class setting who does not learn students' names, who is insensitive to their feelings and opinions or their problems in dealing with the course, or who ignores signs of low morale or lack of responsiveness is performing inadequately in the relationship area.

Blanchard and Hersey (1977) agree that teachers as leaders operate within two dimensions: initiating structure (task), and consideration (socioemotional). They hypothesize that the teacher-centered style, which is high on initiating structure and low on consideration, is appropriate for immature groups or individual students. As the group (student) matures, a more student-centered style, high on consideration and low on initiated structure, will yield better learning. Ultimately, the teacher of a mature group should be low in both dimensions, having moved through a "life cycle of leadership" in the teaching setting.

Although group leadership must include both roles, these do not both have to be filled by the same person. In addition to the formal leader, various members of a group may play one or both roles at different times. To the extent that the formal leader (in this case, the teacher) does not perform both roles effectively, it is likely that informal leaders will emerge from among the group—or that low morale and low productivity will result. Shared leadership in both areas is workable and highly desirable. In fact, one way to alienate group members and create passive resistance is for the titular leader to corner control of the group.

If the teacher as leader of a classroom group assumes total responsibility for the outcome of the group, he or she is unwittingly—through the exercise of unilateral authority—sabotaging its chances of building morale, solidarity, and group identification. The alliance is firmly entrenched in the teacher's ability to share authority, responsibility, and decision making with students (within, of course, the limits of professorial and contractual obligations). Expressions of concern for group members, mediation of conflicts, and interaction of quieter members into the discussion are morale-building contributions that students can also make.

Group-process theory leads us to more implications of shared responsibility and morale. The marks of high student involvement are students' presence in the classroom and their active participation in the work of the group—whether making decisions about course structure and flow or contributing ideas to a debate on the merits of free trade. By contrast, absenteeism is one of the clearest indicators of low morale. Cheating on exams and buying term papers can also be expressions of high teacher authority and low student morale.

Mutual commitment includes sharing responsibility for the course outcome and participating in class discussions, activities, and decision making. This does not mean that there is always complete agreement between teachers and students. They may agree, for example, about the value of certain educational objectives and methods, but not on issues. What is essential is the nature of the *process* by which they attempt to reach agreement. The process must be characterized by negotiation, reciprocity, and genuine interest in mutual accommodation. The alternative of nonnegotiable, one-way rigidity leads to alienation and an adversarial relationship. Classroom task groups, which lessen teachers' authority and strengthen peer relationships, can help students assume responsibility. The assumption of responsibility can make the difference between students' satisfaction with higher education and their disgruntlement (see Kazmierski, 1989).

Curricular and Structural Approaches. The curriculum can be organized to encourage learners to share responsibility for how they will learn, but—with the exception of a small number of innovative programs—North American universities and colleges are organized in a manner that diminishes learners' responsibility. There are exceptions. Some institutions have experimented with structural changes that contribute to greater student commitment and shared responsibility. For example, Alverno College and Moss State College (Bergquist, Gould, and Greenberg, 1981) communicate criteria for mastery to students and then leave students free to choose how to prepare themselves to meet those criteria. The organizational arrangements at Alverno close the gap between instruction and assessment, a system that has been described as the purest form of competency-based instruction. Semester hours are counted only for funding and other outside reporting. Within the college, the entire assessment system is based on four levels of competency in eight areas. Each competency level is gauged by an assessment team, which reports to a campuswide faculty committee. The teacher, without conflict of interest, is free to concentrate on forming an alliance with students and on coaching students toward mastery.

The University of Maastricht, in the Netherlands, achieves a high level of student responsibility by the use of what is called a *progress test,* a repeated final examination containing from two hundred to three hundred questions. This represents the terminal point of the curriculum. According to van der Vleuten and Wijnen (1990, p. 31), "The 'final examination' is given four times per year to all students in the medical school. The same test is given to all students at the same time, irrespective of the class they are in . . . a freshman student will not be able to answer many questions, a second-year student more, and students before graduation answer the most questions correctly." The results of a student's performance over several years form an upward-sloping curve, which reaches the approximate level of a reference group of physicians at the end of the undergraduate years. From the first test, three months after they enter medical school, and throughout their undergraduate years, medical students have the final criteria clearly in mind. This puts them in an excellent position to direct their own studies toward achievement of the criteria. A separate evaluation committee, composed of faculty, is responsible for creating the progress test. Van der Vleuten and Wijnen (1990, p. 28) argue that when evaluation is used for formal summative purposes, "interpersonal relationships take on a different meaning, altering the social structure of a tutorial group." Teachers, delighted to be relieved of the conflicting roles of coach and evaluator, can concentrate on coaching students to pass this exam with the highest grades possible. Students are encouraged to take the exam home and study the areas in which they make the most errors. This has contributed to students' achievement and satisfaction.

Other approaches involve making goals more transparent to learners. No matter how the curriculum is organized, teachers and learners cannot share responsibility for the effectiveness of education if the learner has no idea of the goals planned by the teacher and the teacher has no idea of how the learner is progressing toward those goals (Cross, 1988; Cross and Angelo, 1988). Students tend to study what they think they will be tested on, yet teachers do not always like to "teach toward the test." This gap between teaching and testing presents an obstacle to the sharing of responsibilities and to teacher-learner cooperation. While teachers are busy presenting material, learners are busy "psyching out" the exam. One way to bring teachers and learners into cooperation is to use a device that teaches and tests simultaneously. For example, requiring students to practice critical thinking as part of a learning exercise can both teach the skill and assess it. Cross and Angelo (1988) present over forty classroom assessment techniques that double as teaching tools.

Moreover, goals cannot be clearly articulated unless they are well defined. Cross (1988) recommends a tool developed at Harvard called the Teaching Goals Inventory (TGI), designed to help teachers clarify their teaching goals. She is now designing assessment measures keyed to goals; these measures will help teachers determine how close students are to meeting the goals.

Finally, although the use of learning contracts to encourage sharing of responsibility for learning is not new, recent research indicates that they may provide a useful way to teach students some self-directed learning skills (see Knowles, 1975, 1980; Rossman, 1982). Caffarella and Caffarella (1986) conclude that experience with contract learning helps students translate learning needs into learning objectives, in a form that enables the students to learn them; identify resources needed to accomplish different kinds of objectives; and select effective strategies for using these resources.

Other curricular changes can benefit from student input and shared responsibility, such as the improvement of lecturing and the development of written materials. However, teachers rarely recognize the role of students in these areas. Faculty are usually taken aback at the suggestion that their lectures or course materials (such as outlines and syllabi) could be improved by student input. Yet there is evidence that both lectures (Menges and Brinko, 1986) and the design of teaching materials (Medley-Mark and Weston, 1988) can be greatly improved by the help of student feedback, collaboration, and review.

Conclusion

We have postulated that efforts to improve the social context of teaching and learning should be guided by metaphors emphasizing dialogue and growth, rather than by metaphors emphasizing control and performance. Teaching and learning as cooperative interaction means teachers and learners engaged in direct, reciprocal interaction, in the context of a cooperative agreement. Moreover, the cooperation should be willingly given, without threat or coercion. These conditions contribute to the formation of what we call an effective *alliance* between teacher and student.

The approaches we have reviewed here illustrate the key features of this alliance: mutual respect and commitment to goals, shared responsibility for learning, effective communication, willingness to negotiate and to understand one another, and a sense of security within the process. The transactional approach emphasizes the interdependence of teacher and learner and the unpredictability of the outcome of their interaction. The effective transactional teacher forms relationships that are trustful, open, and secure, that involve a minimum of control, and that are conducted in a reciprocal, interactive manner. Learner-centered teachers share control with students and encourage interactions that are determined by mutual agreement. Teachers who facilitate cooperative learning arrangements model them in their relationships with students. Communication theory focuses on the importance of relationship for the quality of communication and, in turn, the importance of interaction, cooperation, and security for the quality of the relationship. Effective communication also rests on effective feedback. Group-process theory stresses the productivity of a learning group as a function of leader-member interaction.

The significance of these findings takes us back to the concept of the alliance. There is no set formula for the perfect class or the ideal tutorial because, if we accept the premise that every teaching-learning situation evolves through a process of interaction between teacher and student(s), each situation is unique and changing. When problems arise in the teaching-learning situation, the best solutions will be negotiated through communication and reassessment with students. This means that our skills must include not only facilitation but also some ability to think diagnostically about what is happening in the alliance.

In the absence of the alliance, as teachers, we cannot logically know which strategies, techniques, or methods to promote in our teaching-learning situations, because we do not know what the underlying problems in those situations are. Unless we have worked out a way to explore mutual expectations and commitment to goals and process, then any use of techniques is arbitrary; they may or may not work. Students learn how to "psych out" teachers and develop coping skills that will help them beat the system. Students become adversarial and competitive with the teacher and one another. Teachers feel frustrated because their efforts to correct faulty situations seem inadequate.

The alliance implies that we have taken the time to establish with students what that system might be. Rather than attempting to beat the system, students are then an integral part of it. When the system falters, the alliance affords the opportunity to engage in mutual exploration of the process, in order to strengthen it in appropriate ways. Communication, respect, and feedback improve our chances of interpreting the situation correctly, enlisting student cooperation, and ensuring that solutions work. Mutuality, willingness to negotiate and share control, and openness are integrally bound up with the alliance.

Paying attention to the social context of teaching and learning may seem like a ponderous addition to teachers' burdens. Fortunately, however, skills in building the alliance can mature over time. According to the developmental theory of teaching excellence, teachers' development follows the typical pattern of adult development (as described by Sprinthall and Thies-Sprinthall, 1983). Sherman and others (1987) contend that as we develop, we experience growth toward more complex functioning, possession of a wider spectrum of skills, broader perception of problems, and more accurate responses to others. They define teaching excellence as a *stage* of professional growth. Stage-one teachers view teaching as "telling," under conditions in which the teacher has little influence on students' learning. Teachers who have reached the later stages of development regard teaching and learning as a complex interaction of students, course content, and teachers' actions, and they believe that they can influence learning. Sherman and others' (1987) description of a teacher who is at the highest level of development has been echoed throughout this chapter.

In the next chapter, we examine the applied literature related to the social context and offer practical recommendations for creating and maintaining the alliance.

References

Bales, R. F., and Slater, P. E. "Role Differentiation in Small Decision-Making Groups." In T. Parsons and R. F. Bales (eds.), *Family, Socialization and Interaction Process.* New York: Free Press, 1955.

Beebe, S. A., and Masterson, J. T. *Communicating in Small Groups: Principles and Practices.* (2nd ed.) Glenview, Ill.: Scott, Foresman, 1986.

Bergquist, W. H., Gould, R. A., and Greenberg, E. M. *Designing Undergraduate Education: A Systematic Guide.* San Francisco: Jossey-Bass, 1981.

Billson, J. M. "In Search of the Silken Purse: Factors in Attrition Among First-Generation Students." *College and University,* 1982, *58,* 57-75.

Billson, J. M. "The College Classroom as a Small Group: Some Implications for Teaching and Learning." *Teaching Sociology,* 1986, *14,* 143-151.

Blanchard, K. H., and Hersey, P. *The Management of Organizational Behavior.* (3rd ed.) Englewood Cliffs, N.J.: Prentice-Hall, 1977.

Caffarella, R. S., and Caffarella, E. P. "Self-Directedness and Learning Contracts in Adult Education." *Adult Education Quarterly,* 1986, *36,* 226-234.

Chickering, A. W., and Gamson, Z. F. *Seven Principles for Good Practice in Undergraduate Education.* Racine, Wisc.: Johnson Foundation, 1989.

Cooper, J. L., and Mueck, R. "Cooperative/Collaborative Learning: Research and Practice (Primarily) at the Collegiate Level." *Journal of Staff, Program, and Organization Development,* 1989, *7,* 149-151.

Cranton, P. A., and Hillgartner, W. "The Relationship Between Student Ratings and Instructor Behavior: Implications for Improved Instruction." *Canadian Journal of Higher Education,* 1981, *11,* 73-81.

Cross, K. P. "In Search of Zippers." *AAHE Bulletin,* 1988, *40* (10), 3-7.

Cross, K. P., and Angelo, T. A. *Classroom Assessment Techniques: A Handbook for Faculty.* Ann Arbor, Mich.: National Center for Research on Improving Postsecondary Teaching and Learning, 1988.

Darnell, D. K. "Some 'Basics' to Get Back To: A Transactional Perspective on Teaching-Learning." *Communication Education*, 1978, 27, 278–285.

DeVito, J. A. "Teaching as Relational Development." In J. M. Civikly (ed.), *Communicating in College Classrooms*. New Directions for Teaching and Learning, no. 26. San Francisco: Jossey-Bass, 1986.

Erdle, S., Murray, H. G., and Rushton, J. P. "Personality, Classroom Behavior, and Student Ratings of College Teaching Effectiveness: A Path Analysis." *Journal of Educational Psychology*, 1985, 77, 394–407.

Finkel, D. L., and Monk, G. S. "Teachers and Learning Groups: Dissolution of the Atlas Complex." In C. Bouton and R. Y. Garth (eds.), *Learning in Groups*. New Directions for Teaching and Learning, no. 14. San Francisco: Jossey-Bass, 1983.

Forsyth, D. R. *Group Dynamics*. (2nd ed.) Pacific Grove, Calif.: Brooks/Cole, 1990.

Fox, D. "Personal Theories of Teaching." *Studies in Higher Education*, 1983, 8, 151–157.

Franklin, U. *The Real World of Technology*. Toronto: CBC Enterprises, 1990.

Greeson, L. E. "Cumulative (Personal) Record: A Case History in Self-Directed Lifelong Learning." *Lifelong Learning*, 1985, 9, 21–23.

Greeson, L. E. "Effects of Individualized Nontest-Oriented Teaching on Nontraditional College Student Learning." *Journal of Humanistic Education and Development*, 1986, 25, 50–57.

Greeson, L. E. "College Classroom Interaction as a Function of Teacher- and Student-Centered Instruction." *Teaching and Teacher Education*, 1988, 4, 305–315.

Guskey, T. R. *Improving Student Learning in College Classrooms*. Springfield, Ill.: Thomas, 1988.

Hassard, J. *Science Experiences: Cooperative Learning and the Teaching of Science*. Menlo Park, Calif.: Addison-Wesley, 1990.

Jones, J. "Students' Ratings of Teacher Personality and Teaching Competence." *Higher Education*, 1989, 18, 551–558.

Kazmierski, P. "The Adult Learner." In D. Grieve (ed.), *Teaching in College: A Resource for College Teachers*. Cleveland, Ohio: INFO-TEC, 1989.

Knowles, M. S. *Self-Directed Learning*. New York: Association Press, 1975.

Knowles, M. S. *The Modern Practice of Adult Education*. (Rev. ed.) Chicago: Follett, 1980.

Kolb, D. A. *Experiential Learning: Experience as the Source of Learning and Development*. Englewood Cliffs, N.J.: Prentice-Hall, 1984.

Lakin, M. *Interpersonal Encounter: Theory and Practice in Sensitivity Training*. New York: McGraw-Hill, 1972.

Larson, C. O., and Dansereau, D. F. "Cooperative Learning in Dyads." *Journal of Reading*, 1986, 29, 516–520.

Lee, J. A. *Test Pattern: Instructional Television at Scarborough College, University of Toronto*. Toronto, Canada: University of Toronto Press, 1971.

Lowman, J. *Mastering the Techniques of Teaching*. San Francisco: Jossey-Bass, 1984.

McKeachie, W. J., Pintrich, P. R., Lin, Y-G., and Smith, A. F. *Teaching and Learning in the College Classroom: A Review of the Research Literature*. Ann Arbor, Mich.: National Center for Research on Improving Postsecondary Teaching and Learning, 1986.

Medley-Mark, V., and Weston, C. B. "A Comparison of Student Feedback Obtained from Three Methods of Formative Evaluation of Instructional Materials." *Instructional Science*, 1988, 17, 3–28.

Menges, R. J., and Brinko, K. T. "Effects of Student Evaluation Feedback: A Meta-analysis of Higher Education Research." Paper presented at the annual meeting of the American Educational Research Association, San Francisco, April 1986.

Miles, M. B. *Learning to Work in Groups.* New York: Teachers College Press, 1973.

Miller, C. D., Miller, L. F., and Rosen, L. A. "Modified Reciprocal Teaching in a Regular Classroom." *Journal of Experimental Education,* 1988, *56,* 183-186.

Millis, B. J. "Helping Faculty Build Learning Communities Through Cooperative Groups." *To Improve the Academy,* 1990, *9,* 43-58.

Murray, H. G. "Low-Inference Classroom Teaching Behaviors and Student Ratings of College Teaching Effectiveness." *Journal of Educational Psychology,* 1983, *75,* 134-149.

Palincsar, A. S., Ransom, K., and Derber, S. "Collaborative Research and Development of Reciprocal Teaching." *Educational Leadership,* 1989, *46,* 37-40.

Pascarella, E. T. "Student-Faculty Informal Contact and College Outcomes." *Review of Educational Research,* 1980, *50,* 545-595.

Probst, R. E. "Response-Based Teaching of Literature." *English Journal,* 1981, *70,* 43-47.

Rogers, C. R. *Freedom to Learn.* Columbus, Ohio: Merrill, 1969.

Rogers, C. R. *Freedom to Learn for the 80's.* Columbus, Ohio: Merrill, 1983.

Rosenblatt, L. "The Acid Test in the Teaching of Literature." *English Journal,* 1956, *45,* 66-74.

Rossman, M. H. "Learning Contract—A Contemporary Teaching Technique." *Indian Educator,* 1982, *4,* 9-10.

Schein, E. H., and Bennis, W. G. *Personal and Organizational Change Through Group Methods: The Laboratory Approach.* New York: Wiley, 1965.

Schön, D. A. *Educating the Reflective Practitioner.* San Francisco: Jossey-Bass, 1987.

Sherman, T. M., Armistead, L. P., Fowler, F., Barksdale, M. A., and Reif, G. "The Quest for Excellence in University Teaching." *Journal of Higher Education,* 1987, *48,* 66-84.

Simpson, R. J., and Galbo, J. J. "Interaction and Learning: Theorizing on the Art of Teaching." *Interchange,* 1986, *17* (4), 37-51.

Slater, P. E. "Role Differentiation in Small Groups." *American Sociological Review,* 1955, *20,* 300-310.

Slavin, R. E. "Research on Cooperative Learning: Consensus and Controversy." *Educational Leadership,* 1989-90, *47,* 52-55.

Sprinthall, N. A., and Thies-Sprinthall, L. "The Teacher as an Adult Learner: A Cognitive Developmental View." In G. A. Griffin (ed.), *Staff Development.* Chicago: University of Chicago Press, 1983.

Terenzini, P. T., and Pascarella, E. T. "Student-Faculty Relationships and Freshman Year Educational Outcomes: A Further Investigation." *Journal of College Student Personnel,* 1980, *21,* 521-528.

Tiberius, R. G. "Freedom Within Control: An Elaboration of the Concept of Reciprocal Control in B. F. Skinner's *Beyond Freedom and Dignity.*" *Interchange,* 1974, *5* (1), 46-58.

Tiberius, R. G. "Metaphors Underlying the Improvement of Teaching and Learning." *British Journal of Educational Technology,* 1986, *17,* 144-156.

Tiberius, R. G., Sackin, H. D., Slingerland, J. M., Jubas, K., Bell, M., and Matlow, A. "The Influence of Student Evaluative Feedback on the Improvement of Clinical Teaching." *Journal of Higher Education,* 1989, *60,* 665-681.

Tough, A. *Major Learning Efforts: Recent Research and Future Directions.* Toronto, Canada: Ontario Institute for Studies in Education, 1977.

van der Vleuten, C., and Wijnen, W. (eds.). *Problem-Based Learning: Perspectives from the Maastricht Experience.* Amsterdam: Thesis Publishers, 1990.

Volkwein, J. F., King, M. C., and Terenzini, P. T. "Student-Faculty Relationships and Intellectual Growth Among Transfer Students." *Journal of Higher Education,* 1986, *57,* 413-430.

Watzlawick, P., Beavin, J. H., and Jackson, D. D. *Pragmatics of Human Communication: A Study of Interactional Patterns, Pathologies, and Paradoxes.* New York: Norton, 1967.

Wing, K. T. "Implications of Feedback Research for Group Facilitation and the Design of Experiential Learning." *Small Group Research,* 1990, *21,* 113–127.

Richard G. Tiberius is associate professor and deputy director, Centre for Studies in Medical Education, Faculty of Medicine, University of Toronto.

Janet Mancini Billson is professor of sociology and women's studies at Rhode Island College, Providence.

Myriad social arrangements can be created that work toward rather than against cooperation, effective communication, and security in teaching and learning.

Effective Social Arrangements for Teaching and Learning

Janet Mancini Billson, Richard G. Tiberius

What social arrangements are best suited to facilitate teaching and learning? In the previous chapter, we concluded that a new ideal for the social context of teaching and learning is emerging from contemporary theory and research. We described this ideal as an alliance between teachers and students. We identified five key features underlying the alliance: mutual respect; shared responsibility for learning and mutual commitment to goals; effective communication and feedback; cooperation and willingness to negotiate conflicts; and a sense of security in the classroom. In this chapter, we concentrate on how such social arrangements can be promoted, and we offer specific guidelines for promoting the alliance in the context of the classroom.

Promotion of the alliance requires us to shift our perception of the teacher as an agent of change in students to the teacher as a partner in the process of change. Shifting from the production/transmission metaphor to the dialogue metaphor—from controlling or managing students and classroom interaction to forming an alliance with students—is the critical change.

Guidelines for Strengthening the Alliance in the Classroom Group

Katz and Henry (1988) identify several basic learning principles that depend on the social context of the teaching-learning process. They conclude that teaching should be directed toward the transformation of students' passivity into active learning, through inquiry with others in a supportive atmosphere. We have argued that the alliance is central to the social context and have stressed the nature of the teacher-student relationship, but overcoming the sometimes impenetrable wall of students' passivity hinges on development of the student-student relationship and a commitment to collaborative inquiry. This leads us to a model for thinking of the class as a group and for using group activities in the classroom. In this section, we emphasize teaching as group facilitation and group leadership, rather than as one-way transmission of knowledge.

Keener awareness of group processes can enhance teaching effectiveness through improving participation levels, increasing individual and group motivation, stimulating enthusiasm, and facilitating communication in the classroom. Although the guidelines are presented here under the key features they are most readily associated with, all contribute to all features. The guidelines are applicable to our alliance with students as individuals and to our facilitative role in the classroom environment. They can be applied to any classroom, regardless of subject matter or, in some cases, size. They are explicated here in tandem with specific suggestions for course design and classroom management.

The principles of group interaction presented here are by no means exhaustive. Such issues as group emotion, transference (the tendency for students to relate to faculty in terms of feeling patterns developed toward their parents), social control, social status, or numerical propositions regarding group size are not directly addressed. An earlier version of several guidelines appears in Billson (1986); see also Billson (forthcoming).

Mutual Respect

In the previous chapter, we discussed the theory that communication has both content and relational components, with the latter providing the interpretive framework for the former. One implication of this theory is very encouraging. If learning about one another enhances the relational context, and if a better relational context facilitates understanding, then communication should become easier.

Guideline 1: Learn About Students. Teachers who wish to learn more about students should "listen for feelings as well as for thoughts, search for underlying messages, explore thoughts in depth by asking questions, and encourage expression of feelings by showing acceptance of students' feelings" (DeVito, 1986, p. 57). Since most of the contact between teachers and students takes place in classrooms, methods of gathering information during class should not be ignored. The old adage "Start where the student is" bears repeating. At the beginning of the term, three simple devices can help you gain more knowledge about your students:

1. Review results of institutional surveys of incoming freshmen.
2. Ask students to fill out 3 × 5 cards the first week of class, including

name, major, age, career aspirations, current employment, residence, reasons for taking the course, other courses taken in the discipline, and other information of special interest.

3. Allow time for introductions at the term's beginning. Use name tags or desk cards to learn students' names. This is a minimum requirement for classes of thirty or fewer students.

Guideline 2: Help Students Learn About the Teacher. Scholl-Buchwald (1985, p. 17) recommends that teachers "share something about themselves that illuminates their values and styles and cuts through the stereotypes that students sometimes have of professors." He cites an example of a teacher who is bright, witty, and perhaps great fun at a party but who may intimidate students in the classroom. In order to dispel anxiety and improve attitudes toward learning, Scholl-Buchwald advises the teacher to disclose some of his or her own anxieties and shortcomings, or to playfully poke fun at offending characteristics in order to make light of them.

1. Begin the term by asking students to introduce each other in pairs. Participate in a pair yourself. Students can then introduce each other or themselves.

2. Open each class term with a brief introduction of yourself, your research and teaching interests, avocations, and approach to the course and to teaching.

Guideline 3: Develop Sensitivity to Nonverbal Cues. Another way teachers and students learn about each other is through nonverbal cues. Anderson (1986) reminds us of the importance of nonverbal communication, especially in learning about student preferences, values, beliefs, apprehensions, and interests. Nonverbal communication often provides the only data regarding attitudes of students in a large class.

Learning about students implies learning about their immediate reactions to the educational task at hand. Nonverbal cues can be misleading in this respect. Respectful silence can be mistaken for boredom or confusion. Attention to nonverbal cues is important for receiving and interpreting communication.

1. Attend to what students are doing—taking notes, looking at the handout, reading the newspaper. Frowning, fidgeting, sleeping, reading the college newspaper, slouching, and so on, may be as important feedback as that which students provide at the end of the term in a computerized questionnaire.

2. Have a class session videotaped and analyzed with a sympathetic colleague. An informal visit by a trusted colleague who attends to nonverbals may be equally instructive and less threatening.

Anderson supports the conclusion that nonverbal means of communication are well suited to disclosing teachers' attitudes toward their students. Eye contact, smiling, vocal expressiveness, physical proximity, gesturing, and body language can communicate feelings of warmth and support, or the opposite. Failure to attend to nonverbal cues hampers the teacher's ability to recognize incomprehension of or dissatisfaction with course materials and procedures. Students complain that the teacher is losing the class or over their heads. Often, they vote with their feet.

Guideline 4: Establish a Climate of Egalitarianism and Tolerance. Diverse backgrounds and interests can add to the richness of classroom interaction. They can also contribute to misunderstanding conflict, and uneven participation. Students, as people, bring to class their personalities, assumptions about the learning process, physical and emotional problems, and what happened on the way to class. (The same can be said of professors.) Although individuals may coalesce into a group as the term proceeds, this diversity underscores the need for informal preclass interaction, reiteration of clear norms and goals, and mechanisms that foster open participation.

Further, it is the responsibility of teachers and students to ensure that factors of race, gender, ethnicity, religion, sexual preference, lifestyle, and nationality are not allowed to exclude anyone directly or by implication. Inequality in classroom interaction has a poisonous effect on trust. Teachers should endeavor to establish egalitarian norms. The social context will be toxic if discriminatory comments are allowed to float unchallenged in the classroom. Students who feel excluded or slighted are likely to withdraw; both the victims and other students suffer from the loss of ideas. Invite each student to join the dialogue.

Egalitarian norms are as important in a chemistry or history class as they are in a sociology class on minority groups and race relations. Research on the classroom as a "chilly climate" for women indicates that teachers' behaviors that endanger security for women cover a wide range: recognizing and reinforcing comments from males more often than those from females, inviting males to solve math problems on the chalkboard more often than females, interrupting women's comments, making direct derogatory and sexist remarks, and offering more help outside the classroom to males (Constantinople, Cornelius, and Gray, 1988).

A safe climate for learning can be shattered by a remark such as "You girls won't understand this problem." We know of a math professor who taught calculation of the mean by asking females to give their bra sizes. Some withdrew in silent humiliation; others reported him to the affirmative action officer, in indignation. The problem with racist and sexist incidents is that all too many students withdraw rather than protest. Individualization and respect for differences in learning styles are also related to the development of tolerance for individual differences. As students are made more self-aware and respectful of their own strivings toward autonomy, they can also be helped to develop greater tolerance toward other differences that separate them.

1. Do not allow racist or sexist comments or actions to pass unnoticed. Draw students' attention to them, and help students explore the sources of prejudice and discrimination and how these inhibit full participation of all class members and hence the learning capacity of the class as a group.
2. Acknowledge feelings about differences, and create a safe climate for discussion. This fosters individual development as well as group solidarity.
3. Do not insist on a "politically correct" position. Help students explore all sides of a position and understand how they come to their various perspectives.

Guideline 5: Help Students Explore Differences and Find Commonalities on Key Issues. Students who discover, in the process of interacting with others, that their opinions, fears, or problems are not unique are less likely to feel timid in the future to express themselves. For example, a student who feels stupid in not solving an equation may experience a renewal of self-confidence and optimism when others admit the same difficulty. Ask simple questions in response to students' comments, especially unconventional or controversial ones: "Does anyone else ever feel that way?" "Have any of you ever had that problem or experience?" "Do you know anyone who has had that problem or experience?" This last question is particularly useful in stimulating discussion of social issues or psychological phenomena. Students who hesitate to discuss their own experiences or attitudes may be quick to discuss those of family members, neighbors, or friends. This paves the way to open discussion of their own prejudices, fears, biases, or questions.

Guideline 6: Remember That You Are a Role Model for Student Behavior. The leader of any group serves as a role model for its members. The way in which you play your role—including how you present expectations of students, carry out responsibilities, and handle privileges implicit in the professional role—has a profound effect on how students enact their role.

1. Early in the semester, model behavior you want your students to exhibit, particularly regarding punctuality, keeping agreements, tolerating dissent, respecting diversity, encouraging discussion, and being a good listener.
2. Model standards for academic productivity. If your syllabus is full of typographical and spelling errors, admonishments to students about turning in carefully prepared work will fall on deaf ears.
3. Keep ahead of the agreed-upon reading. If you are barely a page ahead of your students in reading assignments, encouraging them to read on schedule will hold little significance.

4. Try to teach courses that genuinely interest you. Students take the lead from you in terms of enthusiasm, energy, and excitement about subject matter. Chances are that if you are mildly bored with the course materials, your students will also be bored.
5. If you expect students to think critically, you should listen to divergent opinions, ask questions, and model critical thinking yourself.
6. If you want students to provide examples from their own experience, begin by sharing an experience of your own.
7. By saying "I don't know" when that is true, you help students to accept the limits of their own knowledge and to admit when they do not know or understand something.
8. By saying "But I know where we can find it," you help students believe that knowledge is worth pursuing.

Shared Responsibility and Mutual Commitment to Goals

As we argued in the previous chapter, an effective social context for teaching and learning is characterized by mutual commitment to the goals, methods, and evaluation of an educational experience. Every participant in a group is responsible for the outcome of the group interaction. A class consists of two roles, in complementary and reciprocal relationship—teacher and student. A teacher may suggest or assign readings; discussion will be vague and one-sided if students do not complete the reading on schedule. The class as a group will be held back from achieving its potential for meaningful and stimulating discussion.

Technically—because of contractual obligations, expertise, and power—the teacher has major responsibility for the outcome of a particular course. Yet college students, as adults (few are under eighteen), share a significant part of the responsibility for creating a successful learning experience. Making the shift from being a passive learner to an active one depends in large part on one's increasing willingness to accept shared responsibility for one's own educational experience.

This is a difficult concept for many students, who have been socialized into teacher-dependent learning relationships in elementary and secondary school. The task for young adults is in large part centered on establishing independence and autonomy from parents and other authority figures. For older adults, highly authoritarian classes can be an instant turnoff—they do not want to be treated "like children." The presumption of responsibility may make the difference between satisfaction with higher education and disgruntlement (see Kazmierski, 1989). Conducting the class as a cooperative learning group, which lessens the teacher's authority and strengthens peer relationships, can support that growth. Group interaction that stresses student responsibility, individuality, and diverse learning styles can reduce inhibition and foster growth.

Student discontent is often expressed outside the classroom and is never brought to the teacher's attention. Students may perceive themselves to be in a relatively powerless position as long as the teacher has the power of the final grade. A teacher who takes shared responsibility seriously and at the same time understands reluctance to ask questions or criticize a teacher's style or methods can try the following guidelines in order to promote student responsibility.

Guideline 7: Share Responsibility with the Learner. Flexibility in course organization and structure allows us to negotiate with each class as a particular constellation of individuals, with their special needs, interests, skills, and prior knowledge. This makes it more likely that students will be motivated to achieve those goals. They will be more willing to take responsibility not only for their own achievement but also for the success of the course. Frequent reference to the syllabus reinforces the relevance of commonly shared goals.

1. Explore at the beginning of each term the concept of joint responsibility, especially with regard to assignments and format.
2. Establish with students at the outset that their discontent, as well as yours, is "group business," and that you welcome their opinions and ideas. This sets the tone for openness and mutual responsibility toward course goals.
3. Prepare a few copies of a basic syllabus. Negotiate details of pacing, structure, and assignment weights during the first week of class. Distribute a revised syllabus the next week. Students feel more positive toward a course when they have had a meaningful role in planning it.
4. Give opportunities for students to plan certain segments of the course, to make class presentations under your guidance, or to suggest and arrange for discussion topics, debates, class speakers, and films.
5. Build in choices between papers and presentations, but invite those who write papers to share their work briefly with the class (or with a subgroup with similar interests).
6. Regardless of subject matter, students can contribute their ideas and information through formal and informal presentations. Simple techniques for facilitating such contributions include asking students to prepare definitions, find answers to directed questions, bring articles or research data for discussion in class, and work in small groups in class to generate questions (answers, policies, principles, theories, and so forth) for classwide deliberation.
7. Check out class sentiment early in the term, so that students' feedback can be incorporated, as appropriate, into the course format.
8. Encourage students to contribute course-structure ideas to a suggestion box, or set aside a few minutes for a periodic check on course progress.

Guideline 8: Strive Toward Balance Between the Socioemotional and Task Areas. As we pointed out in the previous chapter, the functions of any group fall into two fundamental areas: task and socioemotional. Morale, cohesion, solidarity, and effective problem solving rest on achieving a balance between them.

1. Help keep the class on schedule, or renegotiate meaningful deadlines.
2. Help keep the class on task by reiterating agreed-upon goals and initiating periodic assessments of progress toward them.
3. Attend to morale and cohesion by including them in periodic assessments.
4. Maintain good humor in working on tasks. Return to tasks after the use of humor and letting off steam.

Guideline 9: Encourage Emergent Student Leadership. Natural leaders may emerge among students and may function positively or negatively in the socioemotional and task areas. Roles such as joker, clown, negativist, organizer, or class spokesperson will materialize from time to time. As Benjamin (1978, p. 7) observes, "This leadership will encourage or discourage member involvement, form coalitions and factions, or attempt to rule unilaterally. It will operate with, oppose, or act independently of the formal group leader."

Student leadership can help create a strong alliance and contribute to productivity and morale. Nonconstructive, belligerent behavior can be redirected or discussed as part of class business. The teacher who is able to recognize informal leadership and other roles among students is likely to cope better with the class.

1. Notice student seating patterns, and observe informal conversations before and after class. Opinion leaders may be among the dominant participators in class, but some leadership will be expressed outside the classroom.
2. Encourage students who appear to be forming subgroups to bring their ideas and issues to the class as a whole.
3. Invite students who are comfortable with a leadership role to serve as facilitators or discussion leaders in subgroups.

Guideline 10: Build In Early Assessments. End-of-course evaluations may help assess teaching performance, but they do not afford students the opportunity to take real responsibility for the outcome of the course. Administer a simple instrument a few weeks into the course: "What do you like most about this course? What do you like least about it? Do you have any suggestions for improving it?" Responses are written and returned anonymously for discussion and possible fine-tuning or restructuring of the course format.

Guideline 11: Create Opportunities for Informal Interaction. The social climate of the classroom is elevated considerably by allowing a period at the beginning of each session for informal conversation. Coffee or stretch breaks and chatting before or after class are examples of informal interaction.

1. Each day, allow the class to warm up. Arrive a few minutes before class to afford a period of settling in. This is a time when students and teachers can learn more about each other.
2. Help students maintain contacts outside the classroom (this seems to be particularly important in commuter schools) by duplicating students' names and telephone numbers early in the term (with their permission, of course).
3. If logistically feasible, ask students to organize a refreshment pool for midclass breaks.

Students can hide more easily in larger classes, but because each individual is comparatively visible in classes of fewer than fifteen students, pressure to participate is greater on each individual and is also more likely to generate self-consciousness. The smaller the number of students, the more likely the student is to be called on or to be expected to participate. While this makes for a more personalized learning experience, it also may generate or tap into the self-consciousness that some students bring to the learning environment. For the most self-conscious students, building a safe climate is especially important.

Effective Communication and Feedback

Teaching strategies that afford multiple opportunities for individual and group feedback, both between teacher and student and among students, will contribute to a positive learning environment. Such strategies rely on open, multichannel communication, timely feedback, and the open flow of ideas.

Guideline 12: Break the Ice Early in the Group's Life. Some teachers use structured "ice breakers," especially early in the term, to help students get to know one another and to establish each particular classroom cohort as a group. Students will participate more readily when they have been given an opportunity to get to know each other and interact in subgroups before they interact in the group as a whole.

Breaking the ice with simple exercises will have long-term payoffs. Students can get a sense of the communication styles of other students and of the teacher. Ice breakers can be designed to serve simultaneously as catalysts for motivating students to master the course content.

1. Learn each student's name, where feasible, and use it.
2. Invite students to chat for a few minutes with the nearest person on either side. Encourage them to share information, such as why they are taking the course, their major, how they see the course fitting into their

education, their concerns about the course, or other factors relevant to the course.

3. Serve as a model by sharing information about yourself, your interests, your educational and work background, why you teach the course.

4. Ask students to work in subgroups of three or four to define concepts central to the course: What is an atom? What is health? What is crime? What is literary criticism?

5. Ask students to pair off by numbers or by proximity. The topic they discuss is not particularly important. It may be biographical data on the first day of class, or an issue or problem relevant to course material. Give each pair ten minutes to talk. The dyadic form of interaction is less threatening and establishes at least one bond for each student. Then ask each pair to join another pair and share information with other groups of four, then eights with eights, until one large group is created for a class discussion of what was learned in the smaller groups. This technique can also be used effectively with a class of thirty or more, but the progression must move in larger steps until the class is fully merged.

Although even one session of ice breaking will reduce barriers to communication and raise participation levels, shared responsibility and broad participation will be reinforced if students are asked to work in subgroups occasionally during the term.

Guideline 13: Emphasize Two-Way and Multichannel Communication. Boyer and Bolton (1971) distinguish between two types of communication and feedback patterns. In one-way communication, the flow of information is from one person to another (or to a group). This is typical of televised courses and lecture courses (regardless of size), in which the teacher leaves little time for questions or debate. In two-way communication, the flow of information is between and among two or more persons. The sender of a message has greater opportunity to receive immediate reactions from listeners. This is typical of seminars, small-group discussions, lecture/discussion courses, and study groups. (We prefer the term *multichannel* because it implies communication among students that is not directed to or through the teacher.) One-way communication is more efficient—a greater amount of material can be transmitted in a shorter amount of time. However, it is less accurate than two-way communication—the listener's understanding of the information is less complete. The teacher who is geared to straight lecturing may fail to take advantage of the opportunity for two-way communication.

A circle is the seating arrangement most conducive to effective feedback and communication, particularly if the teacher occupies a different place in the circle each session. Other suggestions for creating multichannel communication include the following:

1. Resist the temptation to answer all questions yourself. Redirect and rephrase questions for the class as a whole.
2. Encourage students to comment directly to each other, rather than through you.
3. Remind yourself of two-way communication: "The best general advice to the professor who would lecture well is still 'Don't lecture.' That is, for most of teaching, to think in terms of discourse—talk, conversation— rather than lecture" (Eble, 1976, p. 42).
4. Pause frequently to make sure students are still with you. "Lecturing creates the temptation to set one's voice on 'play' and forget everything else" (Eble, 1976, p. 48).
5. Avoid lecturing from a written script or text. If you do, provide students with a brief outline of your lectures. This allows them to listen more carefully to the flesh on the skeleton and helps them organize their listening.
6. During a lecture or discussion, frequently ask whether students have questions, comments, or reactions. This gatekeeping role also maintains student involvement and responsibility.
7. Allow silence after extending such an invitation. Students in general do not feel comfortable with silence, any more than teachers do. Someone will break the silence and pave the way to further discussion. Goldman-Eisler (1958) found that pauses in speech serve to introduce new and less predictable information. Thus the incidence of silence in group interaction may indicate flexibility in adapting to new situations and elasticity of group processes.
8. Make it a rule never to lecture all the way to the last minute of class, no matter how brilliant your lecture or how much you feel you must cover that day (see Highet, 1976).
9. Ensure that ample time is reserved during each class for student interaction and discussion of lectures, films, speakers, and so forth. This breaks the "transmission" metaphor of information and ideas flowing in one direction only. Even a class of five hundred students sitting in a lecture hall can be given a few minutes (in groups of three or four) to debate and discuss, apply concepts to examples, or clarify terms.
10. As a check on comprehension, ask students to analyze a situation or problem by employing the concepts or principles under discussion. This technique carries the message that you expect students to be active rather than passive learners.
11. Reward constructive participation with affirming comments and follow-up questions.

Guideline 14: Provide Multiple, Timely Opportunities for Feedback. The effectiveness of any group depends on the quality of the feedback contained in the interaction. Research shows that both teaching and learning are enhanced by timely, descriptive feedback and by interaction between teachers and students. This guideline reaches its logical conclusion in the recent trend toward mastery learning (Guskey, 1988), in which students are given scope to define issues, problems, and projects. Work and materials are broken into discrete blocks that can be targeted, attempted, and mastered, with many opportunities for immediate feedback, criticism, redirection, and consultation.

Other research (Egan, 1970, p. 247) shows that feeling-oriented, positive feedback results in the "greatest efficiency, least defensiveness, and greatest increase in participation." This is particularly important in discussing sensitive issues, stereotypical views, prejudices, and values.

1. Build in several points of evaluation, rather than one or two.
2. Return written work and exams in a timely fashion.
3. Remember that not all student work must be evaluated by the teacher. For example, written reactions to literary texts can receive feedback from other students working in small groups.
4. Ask students to give each other feedback on proposals for papers or projects before they are handed in to you. This gives them earlier feedback on their ideas, organization, and direction and helps students develop genuine interest in each other's work.
5. Build in a few minutes for students to work in pairs, giving each other feedback on draft papers or essays. Feedback can be structured in terms of what they found most interesting, what they would like to know more about, ideas for reorganization, further resources, and strengthening the introduction and conclusion.

Guideline 15: Foster Heterogeneity of Ideas. Teaching and learning profit from heterogeneity of ideas. Marton and Ramsden (1988) recommend several teaching strategies that will promote learning. One is to highlight inconsistencies in and consequences of learners' conceptions. Another is to offer new ways of seeing. By building on contradictions inherent in students' views of reality, you can lead them toward formulation of hypotheses, testing of myths, and reconceptualization. It is the tension created by competing or unusual views that makes the classroom intellectually fertile ground. Elbow (1986, p. 41) calls this "cooking." Ideas are channeled into the pool of information, opinions, concerns, and applications that is available for all in the classroom to work with. Elbow says that engaging the "competent, decent" student who is not particularly interested or involved requires this cross-fertilization of ideas and contrasting beliefs that can only come through group interaction.

Heterogeneity of ideas relies on and is a function of open communication. Even though students may be encouraged to feel more comfortable in the process of participating, they may still be reluctant regarding the content. Unconventional ideas and offbeat solutions to problems will emerge only if students feel safe in the classroom. If we want students to share responsibility for the outcome of a class, then it is critical to help them discover their interests, queries, concerns, confusions, and creative ideas. Tiberius (1986) finds evidence that effective teaching rests on meaningful material. Helping students become more self-reflexive in a secure environment helps unlock meaningful material. Creative and critical thinking can be amplified by even participation.

1. Use group techniques, such as brainstorming, to help students uncover beliefs, myths, values, and ideas. This is empowering rather than squelching, if organized effectively. The broader the pool of ideas, the better.
2. Organize a "fishbowl" discussion format, in which eight students sit in a circle to discuss an issue or solve a problem. Other students who wish to contribute raise their hands and are admitted to the circle by those who are willing to give their seats up briefly. This seems to attract students who wish to make only one or two strong statements but are reluctant to participate.
3. Before discussing sensitive topics or solving complex problems, provide opportunities for students to express their ideas anonymously. For example, in teaching the concepts of prejudice, discrimination, and social distance, first ask students to fill out a brief questionnaire about their own ethnic identifications and attitudes.
4. For a science, mathematics, statistics, or research-design problem, ask students to write down their best attempts, even if they seem to be unorthodox solutions. Summarize the results, and present them anonymously at the next session. In this way, a wider range of ideas, values, and attitudes is available for discussion and problem solving.
5. For a history or literature question, ask students to write brief interpretations before the next class. These can be read in small groups, as a way of opening class discussion of a text or issue.
6. Reserve criticism or evaluation of contributions until they have become the property of the entire group and are less closely identified with any single contributor. Soliciting ideas individually or anonymously reduces the likelihood of receiving only conventional or conformist expressions and contributes to the heterogeneity of ideas available for discussion.

Guideline 16: Bring Each Class and Term to Appropriate Closure. All groups benefit from closure. Similarly, when a course ends, the termination process is important for continuity of the learning experience.

1. At the end of each class, summarize the main points of the day and suggest where they might lead in the next session.
2. At the end of each class, say goodbye and wish students a good day or weekend. These small closures serve to increase cohesion of the class as group and reinforce the alliance.

At the end of term, evaluation is a central part of closure. Teachers and students want to know how they fared in the course. There are scores of methods by which teachers can gather information about student opinions and attitudes regarding the teaching-learning situation (see Cross and Angelo, 1988; Weimer, 1987). Student ratings are the most popular form of course and teacher evaluation, but there is reason to believe that direct, face-to-face discussion between teachers and students may be more effective than written questionnaires, particularly in influencing teachers' and students' attitudes toward one another. This means that ratings must be administered prior to the end of the semester.

1. Ask students to engage in an informal feedback session, reflecting on the successes and failures of the course. This may be more instructive than the computerized evaluations typically conducted by departments.
2. Set aside at least one class to recapitulate major points of learning that occurred throughout the term, to reflect on how the class worked together as a group, and to link learning with future courses.

Unfortunately, evaluative information to students is often lacking at terms' end. Papers are graded and left in boxes for students to retrieve during the next semester. Final exams are taken, without discussion of results. Opportunities for self-evaluation are usually absent. Meaningful closure requires some major adjustments to standard course structures (and perhaps to institutional policies).

1. Term papers should be due well before the end of the course, so that information can be given to students in a meaningful way.
2. Give final exams one or two weeks prior to term's end, so that results can be discussed.
3. Invite students to write brief evaluations of what they have learned and what they have contributed to the class. These can be shared in small groups.
4. If time permits, hold a cooperative class party to say goodbye. This leaves a positive invitation with students to continue interacting with both you and each other after the course has ended.

Cooperation

This key feature of the alliance involves moving students from competition toward cooperation. Kohn (1986, pp. 123-124) summarizes a substantial body of literature that points to competition as one of the primary inhibitors of "the security that is so vital for healthy human development. We are anxious about losing, conflicted about winning, and fearful about the effects of competition on our relationships with others—effects that include hostility, resentment, and disapproval." Kohn reminds us about the well-documented negative effect of anxiety on performance. As an antidote, he recommends heavy doses of cooperation. His recommendation is supported by Johnson, Johnson, and Maruyama's (1983) review of ninety-eight studies, in which they conclude that cooperation promotes more positive relationships. Teachers can design classroom structures so that students gain by helping one another, rather than by beating one another (see Millis, 1990).

Guideline 17: Promote Cooperation and Teamwork. It is important to devote class time to discussing these issues and participating in activities that illustrate them.

1. Teach students how to become more aware of their own competitiveness. Inform them about the destructive potential of competition.
2. Shift to process competition, in which students engage in an activity for its own sake, rather than for some product or outcome.

Palmer (1987, p. 25) makes a distinction between healthy conflict and competition: conflict stimulates the active engagement of students in dialogue with one another, while "competitive individualism breeds silent, *sub rosa*, private combat for personal reward." Indeed, he argues that, to sustain healthy conflict, the destructive effects of competition must be reduced by group supportiveness, making learners feel emotionally safe in the group.

Billson (forthcoming) has devised a method of team exams in introductory-level criminology courses. Students work in pairs throughout the semester—reviewing materials, generating questions for class discussion and clarification, and testing each other on central concepts, trends, and theories. The pairs take three exams (without books or notes), working through a standard objective test of multiple-choice, true-false, and matching questions. The two students must negotiate the answers quietly, filling in the computer sheet only when they have reached a high level of agreement. This forces students to think through questions and answers and reduces "potshot" responses. Students also define several concepts and write an essay collaboratively. Under this model, which rests on team cooperation and some mild interteam competition, students' performance on exams is slightly higher than on individual exams. Class morale builds rapidly, teams tend to study harder than many individuals otherwise would, there is more commitment to asking questions about material, and the teacher has only half the exams to evaluate. Students who prefer to take individual exams are permitted to do so, but few choose that option.

Guideline 18: Foster Even Participation Levels. Students fall along a continuum of participation, from high (dominators) to low (quiet ones). Although most students want to participate, it is not unusual for a handful of students (and not always the brighter or best-prepared ones) to dominate discussion. This is true of most groups, unless specific efforts are made by the leader to elicit broader participation.

Although simultaneous talking and interrupting can be signs of a dynamic discussion and high involvement, they can also be used to close out less assertive members of a class. Very early in each course, students begin to be labeled as dominant or quiet. Labels tend to harden unless the teacher facilitates even participation. A variety of gatekeeping measures can be utilized for this purpose.

1. When a high-level participator makes a point, invite comments from others: "How do others feel about this?" "Any other ideas on this question?" "Let's hear from some who haven't had a chance to talk yet" "Are there other ways to look at this? Other solutions?"
2. Use nonverbal cues and body language to invite participation from other students.
3. Make eye contact with quieter students. Shift your stance toward them. Sit next to them.
4. If you use a circle for discussion, change your position each session. Never sit directly opposite a high participator who tends to monopolize the conversation.
5. Establish, with students' consent, a norm of noninterruption, to help quieter students who find it difficult to complete a sentence in an ongoing discussion and who succumb quickly to the efforts of dominants and interrupters.
6. Be cognizant of participation levels in forming work groups.
7. If the problem of a few dominants persists, consider engaging the class in a discussion of how they feel about the participation levels.

Many teachers are reluctant to call on students who do not voluntarily participate. However, good gatekeeping typically creates an atmosphere in which more students voluntarily participate, and in which being called on is not a traumatic experience.

Guideline 19: Work Toward Exploration and Resolution of Conflict. Being able to mediate conflicts and bring debates to some level of resolution is a central role for the facilitative teacher. In virtually any group, differences generate the formation of subgroups along certain lines (cleavages), such as gender, age, major, social class, race, residence, political views, and so forth. Students tend to form various subgroups in class. Efforts to explore and cut across cleavages heighten participation at the classwide level. Activities or discussions that cut across cleavages tend to reduce conflict and increase empathy among subgroups, thereby increasing participation.

1. Find ways to create heterogeneous work groups. You can ask students to count off, or ask students to work with others in their row, section of

the classroom, or year in school. Better still, ask students to select others who they think may have different views.

2. When conflict emerges, invite students to break into brainstorming groups or focused-discussion groups, in order to explore the sources and nature of the conflict, as well as possible resolutions. Groups can reflect new combinations of students for each conflict.

3. When cleavages seem to cluster around two major positions (for example, opposing or supporting gun control, abortion, or intervention in world affairs), organize on-the-spot debates. Make sure that approximately half the class is on each side, by asking students to cross over to the minority position. It can be equally instructive for them to argue positions they do not hold. Give each side ten minutes to prepare arguments and select someone to make an opening statement. Ask students to raise their hands to be recognized, one person per side, one statement per person, until all students on both sides have had a chance to speak. Then ask the class as a whole to discuss the merits of each side's arguments.

4. Ask students to answer, on paper, the question "Who am I?" ten times. Then ask them to form groups of four or five and discuss their responses with each other. This is especially appropriate for stimulating class discussion of such concepts as identity, self-image, personality, and ethnic, racial, or gender identification. Empathy and tolerance may improve.

5. Stimulate debate and dissent while maintaining norms of respect and tolerance for differences of opinion.

Security and Trust

An effective social context requires students and teachers alike to work toward a safe, coercion-free environment. Student participation, performance, and evaluation of teachers are higher when the classroom is safe; when students feel threatened, they regress to surface learning strategies (Eizenberg, cited in Jones, 1989; Numella and Rosengren, 1986). Reciprocal feedback, cooperation, and mutual responsibility cannot occur in a climate of threat, anxiety, and fear of reprisal or putdowns. The alliance hinges on the student's sense of security and safety in the classroom.

In a safe climate, students will feel more comfortable about displaying either ignorance or knowledge. They will also be more willing to share experiences and expertise and to disagree with other points of view. Reduction of self-consciousness, apathy, and boredom will enhance dialogue; participation levels and class attendance will increase. The group climate affects students' sense of belonging and whether they look forward to class, participate, drop the class, or leave college altogether. Safety and security depend on many factors.

Although structural changes, such as separating the role of teacher as facilitator from the role of teacher as evaluator, are important, they require massive reordering of the university environment toward mastery learning or competency-based evaluation. Still, there is much that individual teachers can do to develop trust.

Guideline 20: Make It Safe to Take Risks and to Be Wrong. Svinicki (1989) reminds us that learning is a risky business, and teachers need to support learners to make learning safer. She describes four strategies for building a trusting relationship with the learner: modeling how to take risks, minimizing the pain of making an error, exuding organization and competence, and providing risk-taking opportunities. In practical terms, this may include the following strategies:

1. Work toward accepting criticism of your own ideas or methods.
2. Build in ungraded student minipresentations (risk taking, but minimizing pain of making errors).
3. Take offbeat ideas seriously.
4. Freely admit when you do not understand or know something. This helps students feel safe in doing the same.
5. Help students establish norms of not interrupting or ridiculing each other when they disagree.
6. Avoid personal comparisons as a method of motivating students.

Guideline 21: Keep the Doors Open for All Students. A classroom that is dominated by a few students does not constitute an alliance. It is merely the interaction of a comfortable, vocal elite with the teacher. Others may feel left out and may find it too threatening to break into the dialogue. Work toward even participation, in which dominators are motivated to share classroom space with quieter students, and low participators feel safe to express themselves.

Guideline 22: Reduce the Status Differential Between Teacher and Student. According to Boyer and Bolton (1971), the professor who is perceived by students as having "psychological bigness" inhibits participation and the establishment of a positive climate. Psychological bigness stems from frequent reference to the teacher's high status and titles, a formal manner, displaying an overwhelming amount of detailed knowledge, and using sarcasm, ridicule, veiled or open threats, or terminal statements. These characteristics tend to be associated with domination, rather than with leadership. Here are some suggestions for not outranking students:

1. Resist cutting off questioning.
2. Include and invite multiple explanations of reality.
3. Do not insist that your position is the only correct one. Encourage students to do their own research and exploration.
4. Respond positively to a student's initial attempts to communicate, and

invite further contributions. This will affect whether a student risks contributing again.

5. Respond to all comments. Avoid passing students over. Comments that are not quite on the mark can be responded to invitationally: "Good. Now let's take it a step farther." "Keep going." "That could become important later. Don't forget what you had in mind."
6. Avoid putdowns and close-off comments, such as "You're way off" or "You're the only one who doesn't understand" or "You've missed the whole point" or "You haven't heard of. . . . ?"
7. Avoid sarcasm or ridicule.
8. Avoid making terminal statements, where no disagreement is possible.
9. Before dialogue has passed on to another focus, make healing comments to both sides of a conflict. This will ensure that students are not reluctant to participate again.

Guideline 23: Ask Questions in an Open and Constructive Manner. Another factor in creating a safe environment is the method of questioning to find out what students know or believe. Firing questions at students to determine their level of comprehension is likely to provoke protective silence. Questions should be constructed that encourage students to risk speaking out in class.

1. Begin by asking open-ended questions, or questions that require a group response rather than a single-person response.
2. Reserve a question period. Once you have decided to use this method, stick to it. Do not rush to fill the time by talking if questions are slow in coming.
3. Ask students to try out their questions first on someone who sits beside them in class.
4. Have students prepare questions between classes, which they submit in writing at the beginning of the next class. These set the tone for the lecture and other in-class activities.

Guideline 24: Handle Disturbing Behavior Constructively. Trust and security in the classroom also depend on how disturbing behavior is handled. Violation of classroom ground rules or of basic norms governing social conduct must be addressed if the classroom is to remain safe. Teachers who, for fear of making matters worse, allow one or two students to disrupt the classroom usually create growing resentment on the part of students who are oriented toward cooperative interaction. The majority must feel that their rights are being protected, too. At all times, however, the question of handling inappropriate behavior is a sensitive one.

1. Negotiate ground rules with students at the beginning of the course. Then, such classroom discourtesies as arriving late, leaving early, talking off subject, interrupting, horsing around, failing to hold up one's end in group projects, and so forth, can be addressed by referring the student back to those ground rules, which belong to the group, not to the teacher alone.
2. If disruptive behavior persists, suggest that the class reassess its ground rules.

Security becomes self-reinforcing. Participation broadens as trust increases. As students begin to open up, they discover they are not alone in their confusion or in their opinions. The resulting "all in the same boat" feeling increases trust and participation (Billson, 1986). There are many other devices for creating security, stimulating questions, and fostering interaction that helps teachers to learn about students. For large-group teaching, see Weimer (1987); for small-group teaching, see Tiberius (1990).

Guideline 25: Be Aware of the Development of Group Norms. A group will set its own norms of behavior and will expect conformity to them. These may extend to the teacher. Norms develop in every classroom group. Negative norms may emerge, such as entering late, leaving early, missing classes, relying on a handful of students to engage in pseudodiscussion, punishing "rate busters" who read and complete assignments on time, and manipulating extensions on due dates. Positive norms, such as being prepared to discuss readings, cooperating with others to solve problems, and showing tolerance of diversity, may also develop. In either case, it is more likely that emerging norms will be apparent to the teacher in a safe climate and when channels of communication are open.

1. As soon as you or students notice them, openly discuss norms that work against achieving the goals of the course.
2. Note the emergence of positive norms, and invite students to continue the good work. Chances are that they have also noticed that others are reading, contributing, or showing respect.

Conclusion

Schön (1987) points out the gap between our growing awareness of the importance of social arrangements in the classroom and the actual behavior of teachers. Translating theory into practice, or insight into a dynamic teaching-learning relationship, can be frustratingly elusive. Defining the classroom as a cooperative learning group that is subject to the same principles of interaction as other groups can contribute to our chances of making the shift from theory to practice. The guidelines delineated here can make us more aware of classroom interaction, process, and communication patterns. We can shape techniques of classroom management according to our understanding of group processes, through creating personalized strategies appropriate to subject areas and personal teaching styles.

Sensitivity to group-building and group-maintenance techniques can contribute to enhanced satisfaction, success, and retention by raising levels of both academic and social involvement in the learning process. Social arrangements between students and teachers can be strengthened in ways that foster intellectual and social growth for students and challenges for teachers. This in turn will nurture teachers' satisfaction with and enjoyment of teaching.

There are many roads to learning, and learning is enhanced in an atmosphere of cooperation (Tiberius, 1986). Viewing the teaching-learning process as an alliance, conceiving of the classroom as a group situation, and taking full account of the social context of educational experiences we share with students moves us toward the metaphor of a dialogue and away from that of the transmission of banks of material. A secure classroom climate, in which students help set the agenda, improves chances that they will engage meaningfully in the learning process.

The effectiveness of a teacher's strategy depends on the nature of the alliance between teacher and students. In turn, the alliance rests on whether the methods a teacher chooses are helpful to students, are accepted by students, and are seen by students as the outcome of a caring teacher who is trying to facilitate learning.

How a teacher regards the alliance is partly a function of that teacher's stage of professional development. According to Pratt (1989), teachers at an early stage of development need the certainty of universal strategies. Teachers at this stage of readiness tend to view the alliance as a product of their own good performance. They may rigidly apply recommendations such as those described in this chapter in the hope of making an alliance happen. With luck, if circumstances are right, they may achieve more effective social arrangements with their students. However, their chances of success will be much greater as they begin to learn that recommended strategies, particularly those aimed at enhancing the social arrangements underlying teaching and learning, are not universal but apply only to certain well-defined situations. Knowing when to do what is a judgment that comes slowly, with experience and reflection.

During the second stage of teacher development, teachers shift "from fixed routines to flexible problem solving" (Pratt, 1989, p. 79). Teachers at this stage are more flexible in responding to the demands of the situation with constructions of their own that reflect a sensitivity to new situations. They regard all teaching strategies as conditional—that is, as dependent on the context and the situation. They begin to perceive their teaching situation "as a set of dynamic, interactive variables that require flexible and adaptive use of their existing knowledge" (Pratt, 1989, p. 80). Teachers at this stage of development tend to perceive the alliance between teachers and learners as more than a product of good teaching. They also view it as a vehicle or method for improving teaching and learning.

The third stage of professional development, according to Pratt (1989, p. 81), "is characterized by a consideration of the relationship between social and cultural values and teachers' professional knowledge. . . . Ways of thinking and acting are understood to be cultural as well as conditional." Teachers at this stage begin to realize that their perceptions of the alliance are formed by the metaphors of teaching and learning and by the implicit theories of teaching and learning that they and their students hold. They try to make their theories more explicit, and to incorporate those contextual factors into them, both within and beyond the classroom.

References

Anderson, J. F. "Instructor Nonverbal Communication: Listening to Our Silent Messages." In J. M. Civikly (ed.), *Communicating in College Classrooms*. New Directions for Teaching and Learning, no. 26. San Francisco: Jossey-Bass, 1986.

Benjamin, A. *Behavior in Small Groups*. Boston: Houghton Mifflin, 1978.

Billson, J. M. "The College Classroom as a Small Group: Some Implications for Teaching and Learning." *Teaching Sociology*, 1986, *14*, 143–151.

Billson, J. M. "Group Process in the Classroom: Building Relationships for Learning." In C. B. Howery, N. Perrin, and J. Seem (eds.), *Teaching Applied Sociology: A Resource Book*. Washington, D.C.: American Sociological Association, forthcoming.

Boyer, R. K., and Bolton, C. K. *One-Way and Two-Way Communication Processes in the Classroom*. Cincinnati, Ohio: Faculty Resource Center, University of Cincinnati, 1971.

Constantinople, A., Cornelius, R., and Gray, J. "The Chilly Climate: Fact or Artifact?" *Journal of Higher Education*, 1988, *59*, 527–551.

Cross, K. P., and Angelo, T. A. *Classroom Assessment Techniques: A Handbook for Faculty*. Ann Arbor, Mich.: National Center for Research on Improving Postsecondary Teaching and Learning, 1988.

DeVito, J. A. "Teaching as Relational Development." In J. M. Civikly (ed.), *Communicating in College Classrooms*. New Directions for Teaching and Learning, no. 26. San Francisco: Jossey-Bass, 1986.

Eble, K. E. *The Craft of Teaching*. San Francisco: Jossey-Bass, 1976.

Egan, G. *Encounter: Group Processes for Interpersonal Growth*. Belmont, Calif.: Brooks/Cole, 1970.

Elbow, P. *Embracing Contraries: Explorations in Learning and Teaching*. New York: Oxford University Press, 1986.

Goldman-Eisler, F. "Speech Production and the Predictability of Words in Context." *Quarterly Journal of Experimental Psychology*, 1958, *10*, 96–106.

Guskey, T. R. *Improving Student Learning in College Classrooms*. Springfield, Ill.: Thomas, 1988.

Highet, G. *The Immortal Profession*. New York: Weybright and Talley, 1976.

Johnson, D. W., Johnson, R. T., and Maruyama, G. "Interdependence and Interpersonal Attraction Among Heterogeneous Individuals: A Theoretical Formulation and a Meta-Analysis of the Research." *Review of Educational Research*, 1983, *53*, 5–54.

Jones, J. "Students' Ratings of Teacher Personality and Teaching Competence." *Higher Education*, 1989, *18*, 551–558.

Katz, J., and Henry, M. *Turning Professors into Teachers: A New Approach to Faculty Development and Student Learning.* New York: American Council on Education/Macmillan, 1988.

Kazmierski, P. "The Adult Learner." In D. Grieve (ed.), *Teaching in College: A Resource for College Teachers.* Cleveland, Ohio: INFO-TEC, 1989.

Kohn, A. *No Contest: The Case Against Competition.* Boston: Houghton Mifflin, 1986.

Marton, F., and Ramsden, P. "What Does It Take to Improve Teaching?" In P. Ramsden (ed.), *Improving Learning: New Perspectives.* London: Kogan Page, 1988.

Millis, B. J. "Helping Faculty Build Learning Communities Through Cooperative Groups." *To Improve the Academy,* 1990, *9,* 43–58.

Numella, R. M., and Rosengren, T. M. "What's Happening in Students' Brains May Redefine Teaching." *Educational Leadership,* May 1986, pp. 49–53.

Palmer, P. J. "Community, Conflict, and Ways of Knowing." *Change,* 1987, *19* (5), 20–25.

Pratt, D. D. "Three Stages of Teacher Competence: A Developmental Perspective." In E. Hayes (ed.), *Effective Teaching Styles.* New Directions for Continuing Education, no. 43. San Francisco: Jossey-Bass, 1989.

Scholl-Buchwald, S. "The First Meeting of the Class." In J. Katz (ed.), *Teaching as Though Students Mattered.* New Directions for Teaching and Learning, no. 21. San Francisco: Jossey-Bass, 1985.

Schön, D. A. *Educating the Reflective Practitioner.* San Francisco: Jossey-Bass, 1987.

Svinicki, M. "If Learning Involves Risk-Taking, Teaching Involves Trust-Building." *Teaching Excellence: Toward the Best in the Academy,* Fall 1989, pp. 1–2.

Tiberius, R. G. "Metaphors Underlying the Improvement of Teaching and Learning." *British Journal of Educational Technology,* 1986, *17,* 144–156.

Tiberius, R. G. *Small-Group Teaching: A Trouble-Shooting Guide.* Toronto, Canada: OISE Press, 1990.

Weimer, M. G. *Teaching Large Classes Well.* New Directions for Teaching and Learning, no. 32. San Francisco: Jossey-Bass, 1987.

Janet Mancini Billson is professor of sociology and women's studies at Rhode Island College, Providence.

Richard G. Tiberius is associate professor and deputy director, Centre for Studies in Medical Education, Faculty of Medicine, University of Toronto.

Theories and metaphors taken from the foregoing chapters can shape the way we think about teaching, both when we diagnose traditional teaching methods and when we design new courses.

Theories and Metaphors We Teach By

Marilla D. Svinicki

We began this volume with a discussion of implicit theories and their effects on teaching. The premise was that our choices in teaching arise out of our beliefs about how learning takes place, what motivates students to learn, and what our role is as teachers. Sometimes these beliefs are couched in terms of cause-and-effect relationships, like theories ("Students are unmotivated and therefore need to be monitored constantly, to keep them working"). Other times, the beliefs are like metaphors, not necessarily implying cause and effect but still suggesting actions ("Students are acorns from which we hope mighty scholars will grow"). These theories or metaphors can be damaging, especially if they remain unexamined, because they can cause us to react without thinking. They can also be a source of renewal. If we reflect on our theories and metaphors, examining the assumptions underlying them and regularly testing the effects of new assumptions, we increase our options in teaching.

Theories as a Basis for Revising Current Methods

One use of theories is as a basis for assessing what we already do and making it better. Most currently used instructional methods were not developed out of research and theory. They arose out of tradition, familiarity, or administrative necessity. This does not mean they are bad or wrong. However, if they were scrutinized in light of the theories we have been considering, they might be better. Take the most common teaching method used in higher education today: the lecture. How does the lecture measure up, and how could it be made better in light of the theories we have discussed?

Viewed from the *cognitive perspective*, the lecture has both good points and bad points. Cognitive theory says that the information to be learned must be recognized as important and must be organized for long-term storage. Lectures are usually good at these two things. The lecturer chooses what to include in the lecture and highlights the important points as main topics. He or she also goes to great lengths to organize the information clearly—preparing an outline, developing coherent descriptions and arguments, and selecting relevant examples and anecdotes to make it lively. In fact, this is what many faculty mean by good teaching—the ability to deliver a clear, well-organized lecture. Cognitive theory also tells us, however, that information is grasped most efficiently when it is related to students' already existing organizational structure, and that students need to construct their own interpretations of information, laden with their own meanings, if there is to be effective long-term storage and real understanding. On these points, lectures are often lacking, because they are so instructor-controlled.

Using cognitive theory as a diagnostic tool for improving lectures, we would try to maximize the strengths that lectures have, from the cognitive standpoint, and minimize or fix the weaknesses. For example, to have students construct meaning from the presented content, we could set aside class time for students to create their own examples or interpretations of the lecture content. We could ask students to draw relationships between two or more lectures and then use their ideas as the basis for a synthesis lecture. I leave the derivation of additional examples to the reader, as an exercise in the construction of meaning.

When we view lectures from the standpoint of *motivational theory,* the picture is not as rosy. Motivational theory advises us that increases in motivation revolve around students' general orientation to achievement, the relationship of course goals to personal goals, and students' expectations for success. Since most of the activity in a lecture is from the teacher, rather than from the student, it may be difficult to see how motivational theory applies. Yet we know from experience that some lectures are very motivating, and some are not. The main intersections between the lecture method and motivational theory are in the areas of intrinsic motivation and the correspondence between student goals and lecture goals. Of the former we can say that some lecturers are able to create a state of motivation in the students by their own example of enthusiasm and by using anecdotes and examples in harmony with students' preexisting interests. They also are adept at appealing to certain intrinsic motivators, such as curiosity and vivid imagery. At the second intersection point, we see lecturers who make sure that the purposes of their lectures are clearly stated and that they reflect the purposes of the students. They relate one lecture to other lectures, to assignments, and to long-range life goals in an effort to convince students that it is worth their while to listen to a particular lecture.

Lectures seem to offer little from the standpoint of other aspects of motivational theory, because the theory assumes active responding, something not inherent in lectures. Nevertheless, it may be a useful exercise to think about lectures from the standpoint of these aspects of motivational theory. For example, one version of motivational theory holds that students with a mastery orientation—that is, students who value improving skills, rather than looking good at any cost—will do better in the long run. Is there something we can do in the lecture to foster a mastery orientation? We may consider modeling it ourselves. Thus we would avoid using lectures as polished answers to problems, giving the illusion that one should come up with an answer immediately, without any errors or misdirection. Students may conclude that making mistakes is a bad thing, to be avoided at all costs, and yet we all know that scholarly work does not proceed smoothly, with no false starts or blind alleys. This illusion is strengthened by our focus on the unit test as the measure of worth, a product that displays the ultimate results of learning. Students seldom have the opportunity to show us work in progress or receive constructive feedback on that work.

To counter this image of the product as ultimate, it may be possible in the lecture setting to show students the entire scholarly process, warts and all, as we struggle to answer the questions of the discipline. One instructor of my acquaintance regularly has students bring problems into class for him to work on in front of everyone, problems that he has not seen before. He works them out as best he can, thinking aloud the whole time, so that students can see the process of problem solving, rather than only the appearance of the product. He has been known to invite colleagues into class for subsequent sessions, to work the same problems and then have students compare the different approaches. This exercise demonstrates to students that improving skills, working through problems, is the important part of learning. This should encourage them to adopt a mastery orientation toward their own work.

Looking at the lecture from the *social perspective,* we find the least encouraging results. Social theory admonishes us to make the learning process a cooperative one, a joint effort between teacher and students. What could be farther from a joint effort than a lecture? Nevertheless, the social perspective can shed some light on lecturing, even though it is a fairly nonsocial method. For example, one implication of social theory is that the classroom situation should be a negotiated system that reflects the needs of both teacher and student. Most lectures reflect only the teacher's needs or the teacher's interpretation of students' needs. Taking the social perspective may cause the instructor to make lectures more responsive to needs as perceived by students. This could be done by allowing students more influence over lecture content. A version of this has been proposed by Light (1990) and others, using the one-minute paper. At the end of the lecture, students are asked to write a one-minute summary of their impressions of the main topic of the day and the questions they still have about it. The instructor bases the next lecture on these questions. Another version could have students prepare questions that occur to them as they read text material and submit those to the instructor before the next lecture. The questions then become the basis of the lecture content. This could even be done during the lecture period itself, although that requires an instructor with a great deal of flexibility and background knowledge, who is able to respond to whatever issues students raise. Using the social perspective to modify the lecture in these ways may seem to be far afield from the original intention of the theory but still illustrates how an instructor can use a given perspective to shed new light on old methods.

A shift in theory can spark the creative teacher in each of us, and we need not be tied forever to the same theory. The advantage of theories is that they represent relatively systematic ways of thinking about given situations. With one theory, the focus of a teacher's attention may be on ways of helping students process information and ideas; with another, the focus may be on ways of fostering self-regulation and confidence. These views are not necessarily incompatible; they simply represent different facets of the classroom that figure into the overall design. It is very common practice in the area of creative thinking to ask an individual to view the same problem from different perspectives, as a way of breaking a block on ideas. The same applies to teaching. Viewing the classroom from different perspectives can uncover a whole new range of options.

Theories as a Stimulus for New Methods

Consider how viewing a particular classroom situation from the perspectives of different theories and metaphors helps create new or innovative methods. For example, imagine a graduate seminar with twenty students who meet once a week for the entire semester. The normal way of teaching such a seminar is for the instructor to identify a series of topics central to the field, select current readings that explore the key points of the topics, and either lecture on those readings each week or hold class discussions on them. This pattern is occasionally modified by having each student select one of the topics and take responsibility for presenting a paper on it during the semester. The question we should ask ourselves is why we choose to teach the course that way. What do these choices imply about learning, about motivation, and about the roles of teachers and students? Do we actually hold the beliefs reflected in that course design?

One Theory at a Time. If I view this situation from the standpoint of *cognitive theory*, what would my concerns as the instructor be? For one thing, cognitive theory says that how students interpret the content of the course depends a great deal on their prior knowledge. Typically, the students' background is unknown except for stated course prerequisites and my own expectations about who is likely to be in the class. If I consciously use this theory to reflect on the course, I can move in two directions. First, I can learn as much as possible about the backgrounds of the students and incorporate activities, in and out of class, that will homogenize those backgrounds so that the differences no longer create a problem for class discussions. Second, I can capitalize on students' prior knowledge by bringing it into the classroom and using it in discussions. This would involve asking each student to be the expert in the area of his or her greatest strength, contributing insights and information from that perspective.

Cognitive theory also says that the organization of information is an important component of learning. Typically, as the instructor, I am the one who creates the organization. If I reflect a bit on the theory, however, I may decide to have students create a structural diagram of course content, to which they add new ideas and questions for each reading and class discussion. By the end of the semester, they will have produced something like an organizational chart representing the course, which becomes the basis of their final exam. Recognizing the importance of having students become self-regulated learners, I can periodically discuss the usefulness of this activity and its relationship to their learning. Most important, as I view this course from the standpoint of cognitive theory, I must recognize that each student will learn different things from this course and can contribute different things to the course. The more I allow that to happen, the better the learning will be.

If I think about the same course from the perspective of *motivational theory*, what do I conclude? Motivation theory says that learning is best when students' motivation is intrinsic. Therefore, rather than choose the main topics myself, I engage students in identifying what it is about the main focus of this course that would have the most meaning for them as individuals, and then I structure course activities to include that connection. For example, I could create small study groups, to let students specialize in particular aspects of the content and allow students to pursue their interest wherever it takes them. This method draws on the intrinsic motivation of already existing interests. Motivational theory also says that students who expect success are more likely to work and succeed. Therefore, rather than lecture or conduct discussions myself, I see that students contribute significantly to the class, and I create opportunities in which their expertise is displayed and makes a valuable contribution. Thus they begin to believe in themselves as well.

From the *social perspective,* I need to be aware of the desirability of cooperation, interaction, and security. Social theory maintains that the best method is a style of cooperative instruction. Therefore, I should become a part of the class myself—learning while I contribute my expertise to the group, making mistakes along with everyone else, but recognizing that mistakes are part of learning. I should try to treat students with respect and give their ideas my attention, just as I expect them to give my ideas their attention.

Three Theories at Once. Each of these theories, taken alone, gives valuable insights into ways in which the course can be structured to promote learning. Taken as a group, their suggestions are even more powerful. Here is what I might do in such a class on the basis of combining all three perspectives.

I would decide to structure the class as a group learning experience for everyone, myself included (social theory), in which the whole class identifies three or four questions about the subject to pursue during the semester (motivational theory). To do this, we would begin by clarifying what the boundaries of the content area are generally thought to be by experts in the field (cognitive theory). This would probably be done by having everyone describe his or her own conceptions of what the area encompasses (motivational and cognitive) and then read and discuss an overall description prepared by me or some other expert (cognitive). Each participant would be asked to create two lists. The first would be a list of questions or ideas about the topic area just described, or potential relationships between that area and his or her own specialties (motivational). The second would be a personal bibliography of materials he or she has in a personal library or has access to and that have some bearing on the topic area or on the questions and relationships listed (cognitive). These lists become the topic of negotiation at the next class meeting (social), to identify three or four questions that all students have in common. These questions then become the focus for the remainder of the semester (social). The class becomes a study group of the whole, to search out and share information about that week's question, just as if it were a research group working on a totally new question (social and motivational). All members of the group are expected to contribute to the understanding of the whole (social) and obliged to accept the possibility that the chosen question is one for which there is no answer (motivational). At that point, our task is to speculate on what the answer may be or to suggest ways the answer could be found in the future (cognitive). For each question considered, each participant (including the instructor) prepares a short summary paper or chart, organizing what he or she has learned about that particular topic, including questions that remain unanswered (cognitive).

The instructor's roles include serving as one of the experts (as does each student) and as a senior learner, group facilitator, encourager, and arbitrator of differences. As the instructor, I would also have to evaluate the students, but I would include a lot of peer evaluation of summaries, work contributed, and participation throughout the semester (social). I would also ask each student to evaluate his or her own progress periodically (cognitive). All these evaluations would be considered in the final grade.

This type of class is actually fun to teach. I know because several components (although not all of them at once) have been part of my own classes. The advantage is that I get to be a learner, too. After all, that is what most academics claim to be the charm of teaching: to continue learning themselves.

You may say that this approach would be fine in a graduate course but would never work in an undergraduate class. I am not so sure that is correct, particularly in light of work being done in collaborative learning. These classes, which parallel the foregoing description rather closely, seem to work amazingly well with all levels of learners.

Choosing Among Theories

Not all theories are created equal, to be sure. In Chapter One, Rando and Menges discuss implicit theories, most of which are both homegrown and unexamined, but they are not necessarily wrong. In fact, because implicit theories are shaped through our interaction with the environment, many of their tenets reflect real-world common sense. Ideas like "Students need to know what they've done right and what they've done wrong" are part of most instructors' implicit theories, but that idea also happens to be a tenet of cognitive theory and motivational theory. It is simply a fact of behavior, and anyone who has taught will have experienced it. Where implicit theories may diverge is in explaining why a phenomenon is true or how to tell students what they have done right or wrong. These are more complex issues, and some instructors do not have well-grounded ideas about them. Formal theories are often much more thorough in going beyond simple, commonsense ideas and into these complex issues. That is why instructors can benefit from learning about formal theories such as those included in this volume.

Formal theories tend to be more organized, more internally consistent, and more thoroughly researched than most implicit theories of instruction. Instructors who take the time to learn about formal theories often find support for their own implicit theories. They may also find points of disagreement, but those disagreements should be viewed as opportunities for growth and reflection. Ultimately, no instructor is required to choose among theories at all. He or she simply uses theories as different ways of viewing a situation, in the effort to come up with new and better alternatives.

Integrating Multiple Theories

By now, the reader will have noticed that the three perspectives considered in this volume have one thing in common: all three recommend a shift in the emphasis of teaching, from content and teacher to student. The cognitive theory says that it is the student who is creating meaning and who must learn to regulate learning. The motivational theory says that the most effective motivation is what the student creates, not what is imposed from the outside. The social theory says that the most successful teaching and learning occur in the context of cooperative interaction between teacher and student, where each contributes to the process.

We are seeing research and theory recommending a realignment of the eternal triangle of education: the balance among content, teacher, and student. For a long time, the educational system has been based on a model of learning in which teacher and content dominate and students are only acted on. Even our language reflects that view. We teach the student. We cover the material. We motivate the student. We are the dominant actors in education.

Research and theory do not support that model. The dominant actor is the student. The student learns the material. The student experiences motivation as a state of being, rather than as therapy imposed from the outside. Evidence suggests that this is the better model of reality.

It is gratifying that three very different perspectives reach essentially the same conclusion. Yet each arrives at that conclusion by a slightly different path, using slightly different data, and tackling slightly different aspects of teaching and learning. Each one offers different insights into the possibilities for teaching, but they all fit together nicely and support one another (as we saw in the example of the graduate class, discussed at the beginning of the chapter). They do not, however, make the instructor's job easier.

On careful reflection, the reader can see that adopting these theories puts us in an odd position. We are trying to suggest ways for teachers to affect the learning process, but we have just asserted that learning must be done by the student. This is something of a paradox. If, according to cognitive theory, students create their own meaning, how can an instructor teach them anything? If, according to motivational theory, students are better off with intrinsic motivation, can an instructor intervene without destroying motivation? If, according to social theory, learning is best in a cooperative setting, how does an instructor draw the line between cooperation and the need for authority?

There is no easy resolution, but one glimmer of hope is offered by a careful consideration of the social perspective. An important insight of that perspective is that the instructor-student relationship is a critical one that needs to be a cooperative venture. Whatever is done in instruction should be done jointly by teacher and student. If we look more closely at the cognitive and motivational theories, they make similar recommendations. In each case, the most effective learning and motivation are produced by a cooperative effort between teacher and student. In the case of cognitive theory, the teacher is helping the student to create meaning and to monitor learning. In motivational theory, the instructor works with the student to recognize his or her own potential, to select personal and realistic goals, and to feel secure in the classroom.

This redefinition of roles helps us cope with the paradox. As teachers, we no longer act on the students; we now help them act on themselves.

The theories we have been considering, rather than being in conflict or providing widely divergent views, actually weave a pattern of cooperation into the tapestry of education.

Reference

Light, R. *Explorations with Students and Faculty About Teaching, Learning, and Student Life.* Cambridge, Mass.: Harvard Assessment Seminars, 1990.

Marilla D. Svinicki is director of the Center for Teaching Effectiveness, University of Texas, Austin.

INDEX

ORDERING INFORMATION

NEW DIRECTIONS FOR TEACHING AND LEARNING is a series of paperback books that presents ideas and techniques for improving college teaching, based both on the practical expertise of seasoned instructors and on the latest research findings of educational and psychological researchers. Books in the series are published quarterly in Fall, Winter, Spring, and Summer and are available for purchase by subscription as well as by single copy.

SUBSCRIPTIONS for 1991 cost $45.00 for individuals (a savings of 20 percent over single-copy prices) and $60.00 for institutions, agencies, and libraries. Please do not send institutional checks for personal subscriptions. Standing orders are accepted.

SINGLE COPIES cost $13.95 when payment accompanies order. (California, New Jersey, New York, and Washington, D.C., residents please include appropriate sales tax.) Billed orders will be charged postage and handling.

DISCOUNTS FOR QUANTITY ORDERS are available. Please write to the address below for information.

ALL ORDERS must include either the name of an individual or an official purchase order number. Please submit your order as follows:
  Subscriptions: specify series and year subscription is to begin
  Single copies: include individual title code (such as TL1)

MAIL ALL ORDERS TO:
  Jossey-Bass Inc., Publishers
  350 Sansome Street
  San Francisco, California 94104

FOR SALES OUTSIDE OF THE UNITED STATES CONTACT:
  Maxwell Macmillan International Publishing Group
  866 Third Avenue
  New York, New York 10022

EXCELLENT TEACHING IN A CHANGING ACADEMY:
ESSAYS IN HONOR OF KENNETH EBLE
Feroza Jussawalla (ed.)
New Directions for Teaching and Learning, no. 44, Winter 1990
San Francisco: Jossey-Bass.

ERRATA

Chapter Four of the above volume, "The Transforming of the American Mind" by Henry Louis Gates, Jr., copyright 1990 by Henry Louis Gates, Jr., was printed by permission of Brandt and Brandt Literary Agents, New York.

Pages 3-4:

This biography neglected to mention that Kenneth Eble also wrote *A Perfect Education: Growing Up in Utopia* (Macmillan, 1966) and *The Profane Comedy* (Macmillan, 1963).

Page 75, line 12 and page 81, line 4:

The Perfect Education should be corrected to read *A Perfect Education*.